THE COMPLETE GUIDE

to

CHECK
COLLECTING

A COMPREHENSIVE REFERENCE FOR

COLLECTORS OF ANTIQUE CHECKS, FINANCIAL

DOCUMENTS, AND AUTOGRAPHS

MICHAEL REYNARD

Copyright © 2011, Michael Reynard

Published by
Prospect Park Books
969 South Raymond Avenue
Pasadena, California 91105 U.S.A.

Unattributed quotations are by Michael Reynard

Library of Congress Cataloging-in-Publication Data
Library of Congress Control Number: 2010918489

Reynard, Michael
Complete Guide to Check Collecting : A Comprehensive Reference for Collectors of Antique Checks, Financial Documents and Autographs / Michael Reynard
p. cm
Includes bibliographical references (p.) and index
ISBN 978-0-9844102-5-5

1. Check Collecting
2. Autograph Collecting
3. Financial Documents
4. Authorship—Handbooks, manuals, etc.

Printed in Canada

THE COMPLETE GUIDE

to

CHECK
COLLECTING

A COMPREHENSIVE REFERENCE FOR

COLLECTORS OF ANTIQUE CHECKS, FINANCIAL

DOCUMENTS, AND AUTOGRAPHS

MICHAEL REYNARD

First Edition

Table of Contents

CHAPTER 1

Financial Documents: A Primer

CHAPTER 2

The Basics Of Check Collecting

About the Author

Michael Reynard has had a fascination for finance since he was old enough to spend money. A highly regarded scholar of financial documents, Reynard is a graduate of Stanford University and Columbia University. He currently serves on the faculty of UCLA, where he has an appointment as an associate professor.

In 1999, Michael Reynard authored the bestselling book *Money Secrets of the Rich and Famous*, a collection of financial biographies. *Money Secrets of the Rich and Famous* has been featured on CNN, ABC News, Fox News, and National Public Radio and has been translated into several languages, including French and Chinese.

For many years, Reynard has collected checks of all types, particularly ones autographed by famous personalities. He has also written articles about archival maintenance and storage of valuable documents. Reynard was recently awarded the first United States patent for a card game using facsimiles of autographed checks. In 1998, he cofounded FamousChecks.com, a website that features images of checks written by the rich and famous.

Michael Reynard's writing background, combined with his experience in and passion for check collecting, led to this book — an award-winning guide to the fascinating world of check collecting.

Preface

The wide spectrum of checks available for collecting is truly remarkable. Imagine, for example, holding a check signed by George Washington for expenses relating to his Mount Vernon estate. Or a check dated during the time of the Civil War that bears an imprint of a tax stamp used to support the U.S. Treasury. Or a wonderfully ornate check from the Standard Oil Company—one of the most successful companies in the history of business. These are just a few examples that illustrate why check collecting has become one of the fastest-growing avocations in the world.

Check collectors recognize that a check can represent one precious and meaningful moment in time. Checks provide unique testimonials that illustrate lifestyles and aspirations, and for more routine matters, they reflect personal preferences and reveal priorities, hopes, and extravagances. We gain a clearer understanding of individuals and even generations of people by the checks they write. As man-made devices, they also represent an evolutionary step in financial communication.

In this book, you will discover how checks have evolved to meet the needs of individuals and the economic requirements of business. You will also learn the nuts and bolts of collecting, where to find checks that interest you, and how to evaluate checks.

Check collecting embraces a reverence for the capacity of checks to chronicle human society. This book is dedicated to check collectors and their esteemed value as guardians of the past.

Introduction to Check Collecting

By definition, a collectible is an item whose value originally depended on utilitarian or aesthetic attributes but has since been enhanced by extended interest. For an avocation to have widespread interest, it must focus on a collectible that is available in sufficient quantity, has nostalgic appeal, and has an element of value. Check collecting meets all of these criteria.

The wide diversity of checks appeals to a range of collectors. Some seek checks involving railroads of the 19th century. Some passionately collect revenue stamps on checks, while others pursue forged checks. The diversity of collectors is as varied as the facets of check collecting.

Many aspects of check collecting have educational appeal. Collectors may be intrigued by the two-cent-tax checks issued during the Depression, or by checks issued by famous people, or by the actual design and printing of checks. You don't need much money to get started. Unlike collecting baseball bats, sports cars or antique furniture, checks are compact and relatively easy to store and maintain. Many famous people, including Franklin D. Roosevelt, collected checks. (Following Roosevelt's death in 1945, the New York auction house of H.R. Harmer sold his large collection.)

With a modest amount of money and a reasonable amount of time, you can begin to assemble a collection of checks with special significance. A carefully selected check may represent an important moment in history, may appeal to your artistic sense with its beautifully engraved vignette, or may excite your imagination when you view the signature of a notable individual.

CHAPTER 1

Financial Documents: A Primer

WHAT IS A CHECK?

A **check** is simply a written order to pay money. It is considered a negotiable instrument, meaning that it has the power to deliver a certain amount of money from one who is sending funds (payor) to a recipient (payee). Most checks require that the payee endorse the check before payment is made.

Negotiability can be restricted by amendments written on a check. These amendments may classify the check into various types. For example, **promissory notes** are checks that pledge to deliver money at a certain time. **Cashier's checks** are checks issued by a bank on its own funds. A **bill of exchange** is a check sold to one person for a second person to pay a third. **Travelers' checks** are cashier's checks sold to travelers that require two signatures by the payee.

HOW MONEY, BANKS & CHECKS DEVELOPED

Since ancient times, using written documents for financial transactions has evolved to meet the needs of buyers and sellers. Of great concern to early merchants and traders was a safe and efficient way to conduct business. Transporting gold, silver or currency entailed the risk of theft or embezzlement, particularly when traders traveled long distances in foreign territories. Well-established trade routes were constantly under siege by marauding pirates or highwaymen.

The security risk of carrying gold and silver was compounded by their sheer weight and bulk, especially in quantities necessary for large purchases. So, rather than transporting precious metals or currency

A modern check signed by author J.D. Salinger (payor) to Plainfield Arco (payee), drawn on his bank account at Chase Manhattan Bank in New York City.

for payment, merchants and traders developed a system of written instruments as a substitute for money. These orders for transferring money or credit were far more secure and much more convenient than exchanging precious metals or cash.

Bills of Exchange

A common form of written instrument that was effectively used in local and international commerce was the bill of exchange. Still in use today, the bill of exchange is an unconditional written order addressed by one entity to another, directing payment of a specified sum to a third party, on demand or at a predetermined date.

One of the earliest recorded instances of a written bill of exchange dates back to antiquity. Stratocles, an Athenian merchant, was given a bill of exchange to purchase grain from a trader operating near the Black Sea. His employer, an investment banker concerned with the risk of theft by marauding pirates, arranged for a business partner in the nearby region of Crimea to pay for the purchase. Payment by a written bill of exchange successfully transferred credit to his business partner for payment and avoided the risk of theft.

For many centuries, Venice, a powerful center of global commerce, promoted the use of bills of exchange to conduct business. Beginning in the 14th century, bills of exchange were commonly used by Venetian merchants to protect themselves from predatory neighbors situated along the nearby coast of Dalmatia.

Bills of exchange rapidly became part of international business as the commerce in other major Italian cities, including Florence, Genoa and Pisa, extended into a global network. By 1603, the bill of exchange attained widespread use among merchants and traders in many countries. An example is the illustration of a bill of exchange used by King George II of England. In this case, the bill of exchange directed payment from England's treasury to satisfy a debt owed from a treaty with the King of Denmark.

Later, with the emergence and growth of the banking system, checks replaced bills of exchange as the dominant form of negotiable instrument. Checks were identical to bills of exchange except that payment was drawn from funds on deposit with a bank and payable on demand. Although bank records go as far back as the Bank of Venice (founded in 1171), checks drawn by individuals against their deposits were first known to appear in 1543 in Messina, Italy.

The earliest banks were private enterprises that required the physical presence of a depositor to withdraw funds or order funds on deposit to be transferred to another account. Written orders for payment that did not require the presence of a depositor evolved as a matter of convenience. The major risk to the check writer was bankruptcy of his bank, which would mean losing his funds he kept deposited in the bank.

The city of Barcelona addressed this serious problem by organizing the Taula de Canvi in 1401 as the first publicly owned bank. Located on the eastern corner of what is now known as Sant Juame Square, the Taula de Canvi bank was also the first bank to recognize bills of exchange. The Banco San Giorgio in Genoa, founded in 1407, followed this precedent.

George R.

Our Will and Pleasure is, and We do hereby Direct, Authorize and Command you out of such monies as have been or shall be imprested to you at the Receipt of our Exchequer in part of the Supplies granted to us for the Year 1737, to Issue and Pay or Cause to be issued and paid unto our good Brother the King of Denmark, or to such Person or Persons as are or shall be duly authorized by him to receive the same, the Sum of Fourteen Thousand and sixty two Pounds, ten shillings, in full of the Sum not exceeding Forty two Thousand one hundred and Eighty seven Pounds, ten Shillings, appropriated out of the said Supplies for the Subsidy payable to the said King of Denmark pursuant to the Treaty bearing date the nineteenth day of September 1734

King George II authorizes the withdrawal of funds from the Royal Treasury to fulfill terms for a treaty with the King of Denmark.

The Age of Goldsmiths

In England, the need for a trustworthy private entity for the storage of money was heightened when King Charles I seized the public repository at the Tower of London in 1640. King Charles I was desperately in need of funds to finance war expenses when Parliament refused to grant him credit. Respected entrepreneurs known as goldsmiths emerged to play a pivotal role in public finance and in the development of checks. Thereafter, merchants and traders turned to local goldsmiths to maintain their deposits of gold and silver.

In the latter part of the 17th century, goldsmiths in England retained precious metals for their clients in strong safes. The oldest surviving record of money deposited with a goldsmith is a receipt dated 1633. Their function was similar to today's safe-deposit boxes in consumer banks.

Goldsmiths were the bankers of the 17th century.

In exchange for safekeeping and convenience, goldsmiths collected fees. They often paid interest for money on deposit, and they served as moneylenders at a typical interest rate of 8%. Goldsmiths developed innovative financial instruments to conduct a wide array of business transactions. As early as 1696, goldsmiths used interest-bearing bills of exchange to encourage deposits.

Goldsmiths provided their customers with deposit receipts, also known as "notes accountable" or "running cash notes," that were made out in the name of the depositor and promised to pay on demand. The earliest known specimen of a goldsmith demand note is

Elko, Nebada,_____ MAR 2 1905

The Eureka County Bank

Pay to _Cash_____ or Order $_40.00_

_Forty and no/100_____ Dollars

John his + Bernardo
mark

Checks supplied by a bank that are completed and drawn against funds on deposit are known as counter checks. In this example, an illiterate check writer has signed his name with a cross. His signature has been circumscribed and witnessed by a bank teller.

dated November 28, 1684.

Deposit receipts that carried the notation "or bearer" after the name of the depositor were circulated in public as currency. Third parties could redeem these written receipts for gold on deposit as payment for goods or services. These receipts served as prototypes of bank notes—certificates issued by individual banks for specified amounts that also circulated as currency.

In addition to deposit receipts, goldsmiths began to accept checks known as "drawn notes" from their customers. Their customers initially used these early checks to withdraw portions from their accounts for personal use. These early "drawn notes" were the precursor of counter checks in use today.

In time, the utility of checks expanded to handle direct payment to a third party, known as the payee. Goldsmiths transferred gold or silver to a third-party payee when presented with a written order from their client. Since only the wealthy could afford the luxury of depositing precious metals, it was primarily the upper class that used checks

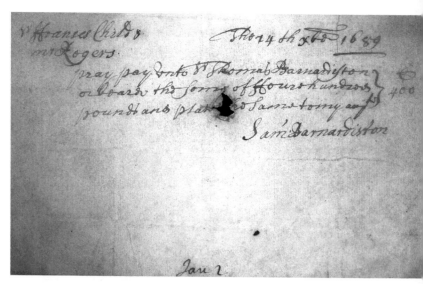

A scrivenor-drawn note from 1689. When the Bank of England was established in 1694, it copied the format of scrivenor-drawn notes for transferring money.

The cancellation of a check written by Percy Bysshe Shelley. Handwritten cancellations of signatures on checks prevented duplicate redemption. Eventually they were succeeded by cut cancellations, stamped markings, and perforations by handheld or desktop machines.

as negotiable instruments in the 17th century. The earliest surviving check of this type dates back to 1670. The golden age of checks blossomed in England later, when the check became recognized as an essential instrument for transferring credit.

Early English goldsmiths were highly regarded for their reliability and enterprise. Their status in financial circles was heightened when the government selected goldsmiths as official fiscal agents, assisting government business and monitoring the quality of metal at the national mint.

In 1665, the English government first issued a form of check known as "order of payment." This government check was essentially a promissory note issued to a creditor for redemption at the office of a specified goldsmith. Setting up this system led the goldsmiths to organize procedures that set in motion a trend for improved checking and accounting.

Scriveners also provided valuable financial services, including mortgage brokering, title searches, and check redemptions. Often they handled particularly large and complex financial transactions. The oldest surviving English check, dated February 16, 1659, was drawn on the scrivener account of Clayton and Morris. Cancellations of checks to prevent their reuse were accomplished by crossing out the maker's signature.

Since goldsmiths were not stringently regulated, they were able to lend money without needing to maintain enough cash reserves to meet the redemption of all demands. Their fractional reserve system augmented their position as bankers and moneylenders, but also led to flagrant abuses and the appearance of unscrupulous businessmen who fully exploited the surging English economy during the second half of the 17th century. Widespread ruin for goldsmiths occurred in 1672, when King Charles II suspended interest payments from the royal treasury for one year. (This was known as the Great Stop of the Exchequer.) This meant eventual bankruptcy for many of the goldsmiths who had deposited surplus reserves under the guardianship of the King; those who got their money out in time, or who did not have deposits with the monarchy, found their competition greatly diminished, and some of them then thrived.

Birth of the Modern Bank

English banks developed in response to public demand for honest, reliable institutions. Robert Blanchard and, later, Francis Child, founded the Child & Co. in 1665 to serve the financial needs of politicians and the aristocracy. They were among the first bankers in England, and their firm made use of drawn notes, which later evolved into checks.

The founding of the Bank of England in July 1694 posed a major competitive threat to goldsmiths and private bankers. Originally formed by a private group of stockholders, the Bank of England was chartered by the government in exchange for an 8% loan of all its original capital to support King William III's war against the French. The Bank of England's notes were patterned after deposit receipts issued by the English goldsmiths and were issued in an amount equivalent to the bank's capital. Sir Robert Clayton, one of the most respected and successful scrivener bankers, served as director of the Bank of

England from 1702 until his death in 1707.

Bank of England currency initially consisted of handwritten notes imprinted with the bank's name. Until fully printed currency was issued in 1855, each Bank of England note was individually signed, and the cashier filled in the name of the payee. Essentially, these early bank notes were checks written by the bank for customers to draw from their individual accounts.

The Bank of England, with government backing, replaced English goldsmiths as the government's official fiscal agents and soon grew to a respected and powerful position. Moreover, unlike the goldsmiths, the Bank of England was prohibited from advancing more money than it held in capital reserves.

Deposits held by the Bank of England included vast stockpiles of gold belonging to English royalty. Bank notes backed by enormous gold reserves allowed the bank to eclipse drawn notes issued by goldsmiths and bank notes from private banks. In addition, government acts of 1708 and 1709 prohibited entities of fewer than six people from organizing banks or issuing bank currency. With its strong monopolistic financial position, the Bank of England was able to lend money at interest rates lower than its competitors.

The Check is Born

In response to this growing domination, goldsmiths, scriveners, and private banks promoted the use of printed checks to compete with bank notes issued by the Bank of England. The term "check" began to be commonly used about 1720, and printed checks were seen more often by the 1750s. By 1800 there were about 70 banks in London that redeemed checks, and printed checks were the norm for the wealthy. Depositors with checking privileges continued to patronize goldsmiths and so-called "country banks" outside of London, where the Bank of England did not establish branches until after the financial crisis of 1825.

The convenience of check writing coupled with the safety of deposits held by goldsmiths and private banks permitted them to accumulate deposits, which provided capital for profitable lending. By the end of the 18th century, many private banks in London ceased issuing bank notes and relied exclusively on the check system to encourage deposits. Checks were now commonly used in England for making deposits and transferring funds from one private bank to another. The Bank of England began to issue checkbooks in 1830. The 18th century saw universal recognition and acceptance of checks as financial instruments.

Competition with the Bank of England caused goldsmiths and private bankers to ease money-lending criteria, enabling generous loans for industrial development. Enormous amounts of capital for financing applications involving steam engines and other new inventions were needed.

The increased use of check-writing deposit accounts provided the reserves needed by goldsmiths and private banks to increase their lending, and that financing fueled an explosive growth of technology as part of England's Industrial Revolution. In this context, deposits held by check-writing accounts helped shape England's tremendous economic expansion from 1760 to 1840.

It was greater competition among banks for customer deposits that led to affordable banking. By the turn of the 18th century, individuals from all sorts of economic backgrounds, including those of lesser means, began to use deposit banking and check writing for personal and business purposes. As checks gained in popularity, many wealthy individuals delegated the task of check writing to bookkeepers and business managers.

Check writing reached another pinnacle when the Royal Bank of Scotland, founded in 1727, introduced the bank overdraft. The overdraft was a radical departure from the commonly accepted principle of maintaining full reserves to cover all potential withdrawals. Now the bank could convert a check into a profitable short-term loan.

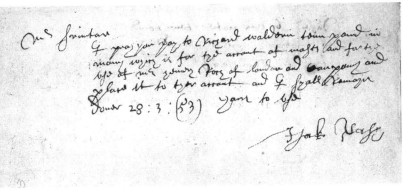

This handwritten manuscript check, believed to be the oldest existing check from North America, was drawn on a branch of London and Company on March 23, 1653.

Early Banking in America

In early America, checks drawn from bank accounts were preceded by bills of exchange drawn on English holding companies. Since overseas business transactions were at high risk of loss by theft or shipwreck, colonists often sent up to four bills of exchange, via different routes, in hopes that one would successfully arrive at its destination.

John Jacob Astor, a highly successful American businessman, was less confident for a successful delivery when he wrote his fourth bill of exchange to his agent in Amsterdam.

Early American colonists had very little money to deposit with holding companies or banks. Exportation of currency from England had been prohibited since 1695, and English law forbade the colonies from producing currency. This prohibition became a major factor leading to the Revolutionary War.

The first experience with checks in America occurred with an experimental financial arrangement known as "The Fund at Boston in New England." Boston businessmen mortgaged their land and possessions for credit used against their checks. However, it was only with the development of deposit banking after the Revolutionary War that checking became widespread.

While advocating political separation from England, John Hancock asked a London merchant to pay his English agent on his first bill of exchange if his second and third bills of exchange had not been redeemed. Two years later, John Hancock became the first person to sign the Declaration of Independence.

John Jacob Astor's fourth bill of exchange instructs a payee in Amsterdam to remit payment if three prior attempts remain unpaid.

Promissory notes were commonly accepted as instruments for transfer of credit in the young America. Unlike a check, which involves a bank, a promissory note is an unconditional promise by the maker to pay on demand, or at a certain future time, a sum of money to the order or bearer of the note. Promissory notes were often endorsed from one person to another as a means of payment.

A promissory note written by Robert Morris to his business associate John Nicholson.

Robert Morris played an important role in the development of banking and check writing in America. After his appointment as superintendent of finance on February 18, 1781, Morris organized the first central bank in America, the Bank of North America. This bank restored economic stability when the possibility of bankruptcy arising from Revolutionary War debts threatened the economic viability of the incipient nation. The Bank of North America was also the first bank in the United States to redeem checks for funds held on deposit. During this period, printed checks were used for the first time in America.

Three years later, Alexander Hamilton founded the Bank of New York, the oldest continually operating bank and checking institution in America.

With the emergence of reputable banks in America, early colonists were encouraged to establish deposit accounts that checks could draw from. Pay orders drawn from deposits held by a state treasury were commonly used.

After the charter for the second Bank of the United States expired in 1816, the federal government supported and encouraged the growth of state-chartered banks.

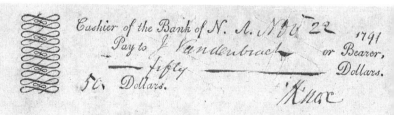

The Bank of North America was America's first formal bank and first incorporated stockholder-owned business. Subscriptions to purchase up to 1,000 shares of its stock at $400 a share were America's first initial public offering. Founded in 1781, the bank functioned primarily as a vehicle for financing the American Revolution. The serpentine pattern along the left margin is one of the earliest decorative designs printed on American checks. Checks from the Bank of North America were the first checks in America that were printed with the word "Dollars."

Founded in 1784 by Alexander Hamilton, the Bank of New York is the oldest continually operating bank in the United States.

Handwritten pay orders such as this were drawn on the state treasury of Connecticut to pay soldiers serving in the state militia during the Revolutionary War.

Public acceptance and usage of checks expanded as the number of state chartered banks grew from 28 in 1800 to 307 by 1820. However, state-chartered banks were not well regulated and were therefore fraught with incompetence and corruption.

As a result of fraud, the Farmers Exchange Bank of Gloucester, Rhode Island, founded in 1804, became the first of a succession of failed banks. Shortly before closing its doors, it had $580,000 in bank notes in circulation—but they were backed by only $8,648 in deposits. The lack of safety for bank depositors dampened the growth of banking and check writing during this time.

As a means to bolster public confidence, banks started creating exquisite engravings on their checks to enhance their image as financially sound and reliable institutions. Furthermore, from the 1800s until 1933, checks could be redeemed for gold or silver, which were universally accepted over paper currency as a secure and trusted standard of value and wealth.

The diversity of bank notes issued by individual state banks was another significant fiscal problem. Lack of uniformity of currency impaired interstate commerce and caused a variety of other issues. In response, Congress passed two important laws that greatly influenced the direction and growth of banking and check writing.

William Colwell, Judge John Harris and nine other directors of the Farmers Exchange Bank of Gloucester, Rhode Island, withdrew checking account deposits and precious-metal holdings from their bank and replaced them with their own promissory notes. The bank also issued $580,000 in its own currency to mask the fact that it did not have enough funds on deposit. Having begun with a capitalization of $100,000, the bank was left with a mere $45 when it abruptly closed its doors in 1809—the first bank failure in America.

Prior to 1933, checks drawn on banks in the United States could be redeemed for gold or silver. Gold bullion deposits at the New York Federal Reserve, Fort Knox and the Bank of England contain the largest repositories of gold in the world. This check from 1876 was paid with $600 worth of gold on the account of Kountze Brothers in New York City to Wau Yuen & Company in Helena, Montana.

The first was the National Bank Act of 1863. It required nationally chartered banks to issue a uniform type of currency. Two years later, Congress levied a 10% tax on currency issued by state-chartered banks to further encourage a uniform system of currency. These economic disincentives effectively shattered the system of state-bank currencies and reduced the number of state banks from 1,527 in 1860 to 247 in 1868. In the meantime, the number of national banks more than tripled.

State banks that issued notes that exceeded reserves often led to precarious financial positions and occasional bankruptcies. Check writers who lost their deposits when banks failed turned to private hoarding of money. The New York Public Safety Fund Law of 1829 was the first organized banking insurance to address this problem. Each participating bank contributed to a fund that paid the obligations of failed banks. Independent commissioners conducted audits of each bank's operations at least four times a year. This ambitious undertaking was the first supervisory program of banking activity in America. In 1837, Virginia became the first state to legally require a bank to hold a percentage of reserves against its bank notes.

Paradoxically, the effect of congressional legislation in the 1800s led to a boom in check writing necessary for the survival of state banks. For state-chartered banks to prosper, they needed to use checks as effective substitutes for local bank currency. Customers of state banks were encouraged to write checks as a means of payment rather than pay taxes for transactions involving bank notes.

The number of state-chartered banks rebounded as the popularity of check writing increased. State deposit funds that bolstered confidence coupled with the convenience of check writing meant that by 1838, almost all payments in the United States, except minor retail transactions, were made by checks. By 1871, primarily because of checking activity, the deposits of state

By the time of the American Civil War, there were 1,600 banks in the United States issuing about 7,000 different types of bank notes.

banks were equivalent to those of national banks. However, with a financial drain imposed by the Civil War (1861-1864), checks and other fiscal documents became a target for fundraising to bolster government coffers.

Revenue Stamps

By 1865, United States Treasury revenues were $334 million, and the federal deficit approached $1 billion. New laws mandated the use of revenue stamps on a variety of financial documents to generate revenue for the U.S. Treasury. During the Civil War, the Confederate states did not issue revenue stamps—this was a Union venture.

With few exceptions, effective October of 1862, the federal government required all bank checks, drafts and pay orders for any amount over $20 to have affixed revenue stamps to show proof of tax payment. Financial documents for more than $20 without stamps were not acceptable as negotiable instruments and were not admissible in legal matters.

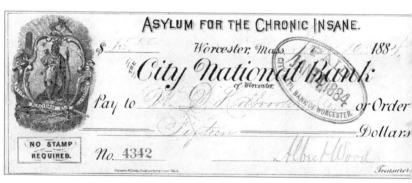

Beginning October 1, 1862, federal law required that people pay a tax on checks and other financial documents. A revenue stamp provided proof that the tax was paid. Checks originating from federal, state or municipal institutions were exempt from revenue stamp tax. This check is marked "No Stamp Required" because of its tax-exempt status.

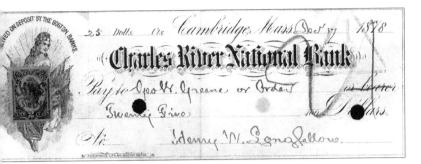

American poet H.W. Longfellow affixed the required revenue stamp documenting his payment of taxes. His initials and date served as a form of cancellation that prevented the revenue stamp from being reused.

In all cases where an adhesive revenue stamp was used, the maker of the check was required to write or imprint in ink his initials and the date in a legible manner.

Later, in August of 1864, a new revenue law mandated a two-cent tax on all checks and drafts, regardless of the amount of transaction. As a result, banks often imprinted revenue stamps directly on checks or drafts. Checks with these imprinted revenue stamps did not require loose stamps, which needed to be licked and laboriously affixed on checks. In addition, having checks with imprinted revenue stamps prevented fraudulent reuse of loose stamps. The American Phototype Company in New York City was the first company authorized and subsidized by the U.S. government to print revenue stamps on documents.

The government abolished taxes requiring revenue stamps on checks on July 1, 1883, but they returned from 1898 to 1901, to raise money to defray the cost of the Spanish American War.

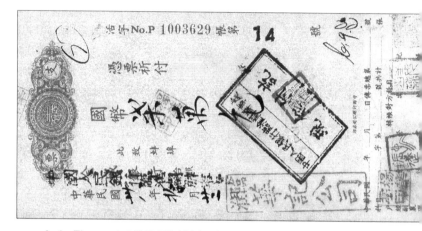

In the T'ang period (616-906 AD), bankers in the Sich'uan province of China distributed paper money and issued checks centuries before such a system was adopted in the West. Since 1986, the year of the first Chinese credit card, check writing has seen a revival in popularity. This 1938 check was drawn on the Bank of China, the second largest bank in China and one of many Chinese state banks with combined deposits of more than $800 billion. Billions of financial transactions are conducted each year by checks drawn on Chinese banks.

Clearinghouses Arrive

With the proliferation of worldwide banking, particularly in America and England, checks became the primary means by which payments were made and credit transfer accomplished. Bank drafts were extensively used as an order for one bank to direct a correspondent bank to make payment to a third party. Banks in small cities often had correspondent banks in large cities to remit funds over great distances.

As checks gained in popularity, an organized structure known as the clearinghouse system became necessary for banks and their branches to exchange checks, settle balances, and reconcile accounts. This system had its roots in an informal system in England, in which bank clerks met at a coffeehouse to exchange checks drawn on their respective banks. By 1773, this clearinghouse system had become a routine method of business, and by 1810, the London Clearinghouse had 46 members. The first American clearinghouse for checks was established October of 1853 in New York. Soon, more appeared in Boston (1855), Philadelphia (1858), Cleveland (1850), and San Francisco (1876).

In other countries, clearinghouses developed much later. It was not until the late 1800s that France established them, after the country began to legally recognize checks in 1865. Clearinghouses to reconcile bank checking accounts in Paris and Vienna came along in 1872.

Clearinghouses settled accounts by debiting and crediting bank accounts. Checks were not "paid" by exchanging checks or by remitting hard currency, but rather by debiting and crediting bank deposits. In America, member banks of an association issued "Clearing House Certificates" to expedite the settlement of accounts between its members. These certificates served to credit and debit accounts of the various members of a clearinghouse.

Clearing House Certificates were either notes issued on the credit of a clearinghouse, printed denomination notes issued by a bank, or "payroll checks" by a depositor in a specific bank. Clearing House Certificates were used in 1857, 1873, 1884, 1890, 1893, 1907-08, 1914, and 1933. Many of these certificates were destroyed after they were no longer needed. Clearing House Certificates are now rarely seen and are avidly sought by collectors.

With increasing need for regulation and expedient processing, the United States Congress created the Federal Reserve System, which officially began on December 23, 1913, when President Woodrow Wilson signed the Owen-Glass Act into law. The Federal Reserve insured bank deposits and organized a system of twelve district branches across America to expedite the collection and clearing of checks between its member banks. Participation in the Fed system precluded member banks from levying remittance charges for check processing.

The Federal Reserve Bank of Atlanta: Birminham, Alabama branch. Federal Reserve banks handle about 27% of U.S. checks.

After the devastation of the stock market crash of 1929 and the subsequent bank failures, the Banking Act of 1933 created the Federal Deposit Insurance Corporation (FDIC). Despite opposition from many leading politicians and the Roosevelt administration, this legislation was brought to fruition by public demand. With government insurance protecting bank holdings, customers gradually became more likely to open, retain, and add to their checking accounts.

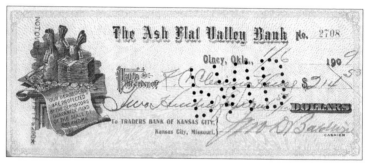

Banks applied exquisite engravings on their checks to portray financial strength, instill consumer confidence, and encourage deposits. This ornately engraved check also assures depositors that their funds are protected by the State Bank of Oklahoma insurance fund. The first organized banking insurance in America was established by the New York Safety Fund Law in 1829. In 1933, the Federal Reserve Bank, the central bank of the United States, created the Federal Deposit Insurance Corporation to insure checking and savings deposits of member banks.

Rules, Regulations & Security

Rules governing financial transactions, including checking accounts, bank deposits, and collections, developed over the centuries as a matter of custom and utility. In America, the states gradually adopted a group of regulations known as the Uniform Commercial Code, to clarify and modernize regulations governing business transactions. Initially enacted in Pennsylvania in 1952 and then by every state and territory except Louisiana and Puerto Rico, the Uniform Commercial Code provides rules and principles for most aspects of business, including transactions executed by checks.

Next to cash, check writing became the dominant instrument for performing financial transactions in the 1930s and '40s, and the number of checks written every year surged to tremendous levels. Banks closed their doors at 2 p.m. ("Banker's Hours") every day so the staff would have time to process checks and maintain account balances.

Between 1943 and 1952, the number of checks written annually skyrocketed from 4 billion to 8 billion. Banks were barely able to keep pace with the staggering level of labor and paperwork needed to process so many checks. In the early 1950s, the banking industry faced a threatening crisis.

Enter MICR (Magnetic Ink Character Recognition)

Bank of America, the largest bank in the world in the 1950s, understood the importance of developing an automated check-handling system and improving the efficiency of check processing. In the '50s, the number of checking accounts at its branches was increasing at the rate of 23,000 per month. Unless they developed an automated and cost-effective processing system, bank clerks would be buried under a mountain of paperwork and corporate growth would come to a grinding halt.

Bank of America contracted with the Stanford Research Institute (SRI) in Palo Alto, California to develop a computerized system capable of rapid and accurate check processing. In a project financed by the bank and shrouded in secrecy, 35 principal engineers at SRI developed a functional prototype check-handling system. It contained a large vacuum tube computer, a high-speed check sorter, and a terminal at which human operators imprinted bar codes to identify customer account numbers and check amounts. Bank of America formally announced its new automated check processing system based on barcode data entry on September 22, 1955.

Bar coding, however, had significant limitations. While legible to a computer, it could not be read with accuracy by a human. In addition, bar code reading at that time was notoriously inaccurate, with an error rate estimated to be 3.5% to 5.7%.

Magnetic Ink Character Recognition (MICR) allows a check to be read by both people and machines. Its font system resists misinterpretation, even when the printed patterns are obscured by ink or pencil. This check was processed even though Frank Sinatra's signature covered part of the MICR line.

Around the same time, SRI had also initiated a research program under the direction of Dr. Kenneth Eldredge to develop a data entry technique for checks that was readable by both people and machines. Optical character recognition (OCR) was not suitable because smudged checks or writing over characters produced an unacceptable error rate. Eldredge came up with the idea of using magnetic ink in combination with a uniquely shaped character font and a special character reader to solve this critical problem.

The magnetic character system invented in 1961 by Eldredge (United States patent number 3,000,000) was called Magnetic Ink Character Recognition (MICR.) Experts have touted the MICR system as the biggest single advance in the history of banking.

When Bank of America invited the business-machine industry to submit bids for making the SRI prototype into a workable system, traditional members of the industry balked. Instead of taking the risk of developing systems that used MICR, National Cash Register and other companies recommended revisions in their existing equipment.

General Electric, a company with neither banking knowledge nor experience manufacturing business equipment but one rich in engineering and scientific talent, recognized the opportunity in the new field of data entry. GE won Bank of America's $35 million contract to manufacture 30 so-called ERMA (Electronic Recording Method of Accounting) systems capable of automating the demand deposit system of the bank's branches throughout California.

This new system used inks containing magnetic iron oxide, a material pioneered and patented by Jacob Snoek of Einthoven Labs of Phillips Corporation in Holland for use with magnetic tape, to print an alphanumeric code on the front of checks. Magnetic ink printing was inexpensive and was not easily obscured by smudges, stamp cancellations and pen marks.

Standardized impressions with magnetic iron oxide ink consist of alphanumeric characters printed one-eighth inch apart on a 0.625-inch high line positioned at a specific level above the bottom edge of a check. Eventually, scanning machines reading magnetic iron oxide characters became capable of processing more than 2,400 checks a minute with an astonishing level of accuracy; each is coded with the bank routing number, the check writer's account number and the check number.

A more recent development is point of sale terminals that can read MICR numbers on checks and provide immediate verification that the writer has sufficient funds on deposit to cover the purchase.

The computer system for electronic check processing was the first transistorized commercial computer system produced in any appreciable volume. By 1967, virtually every check in America and many foreign countries was printed with MICR.

The ERMA sorter, invented by Kenneth Eldredge (above), was developed as a joint project at Stanford Research Institute. Photo: SRI.

Implementation of MICR and other check-handling innovations developed at SRI and GE (under the auspices of Bank of America) made it possible for banks to accurately handle the burgeoning num-

This original laboratory prototype for electronic check processing was constructed at the Stanford Research Institute in Palo Alto, California. It had many racks of vacuum tubes and reels of magnetic tape. Photo: Bank of America Archives.

ber of checks in the latter half of the 20th century. Thanks to MICR, annual check processing in America grew from 5.3 billion checks in 1945 to 42.5 billion in 2004. Former president Ronald Reagan observed that the implementation of "ERMA to the world literally saved the banking industry from drowning in paper."

At first, only specialized form printers were capable of printing MICR checks. However, as the cost of MICR printers has come down, large companies that produce large quantities of checks are now able to print their own MICR checks.

In 1980, the Xerox Corporation introduced the first printer (model 9790) using xerographic dry-powder toner for laser MICR check printing—and several years later, when desktop computers arrived, this technology allowed anyone to print negotiable MICR checks.

Desktop machines using MICR toner cartridges are able to print checks at a cost less than one-half of similar checks obtained from a printer. Desktop check printing omits the need for check storage and provides immediate accessibility.

A major limitation that hinders high-speed check processing is the manual input needed to key in handwritten amounts, but that situation is improving. High-speed video scanners now store images of handwritten amounts in algorithmic equations, which can be translated into digital data suitable for rapid computer processing. Scanning of checks coupled with algorithmic handwriting conversion allows for the practical compression of check data and the display of checks on a bank terminal or home computer, instantaneously and in color or black and white.

Computerized handling of checks by the Federal Reserve currently provides the vast bulk of U.S. check processing. The Fed processes more than 60,000 checks every hour, and it also operates Fedwire, one of the busiest computer networks in the world, handling more than $1 trillion dollars every day. Member banks of the Federal Reserve System use this clearing service at no charge. The full cost of processing a check is estimated to be between 40 and 90 cents each; the cost to run this entire processing system is several billion dollars annually.

The Federal Reserve Bank employs about 5,000 people to handle checks and uses Fedwire to process an average of 150,000 interbank transactions every minute, including more than 2 billion checks daily by more than 14,000 American banks. Fed member banks depend on Fedwire to transfer vast sums of money and accurately reconcile account balances.

Citibank, America's largest bank, uses Fedwire to clear as much as $50 billion in checks with overnight processing. Fedwire also permits the Federal Reserve Board to scrutinize unusually large transfers of money, as part of the search for illegal transactions and money laundering.

Clearance systems in European countries also rely on electronic mechanisms to transfer tremendous amounts of money. In Great Britain, the combined clearance systems account for $200 billion per day, and the Swiss Interbank Clearing System processes $135 billion daily. The Cheque and Credit Clearing Company (C&CCC) manages the clearing of checks in England, under the direction of the Association for Payment Clearing Services (APACS). About 12 million checks are written in Great Britain each working day.

About 70% to 80% of all money held by Americans is deposited in checking accounts. In addition, some 90% of the monetary value of all transactions is conducted with checks. American individuals and businesses write about 42.5 billion checks every year. Since the 1850s, checks have maintained an unchallenged and privileged status as the world's premier instrument for conducting financial transactions.

MONEY & CHECKS: THE FUTURE

It seems clear that the preeminent position checks have held in the world of financial transactions in the world is peaking. Since the 1960s, observers have written about a "checkless" or "cashless" society, one in which electronic transactions by debit and credit cards, telephonic keypads, automated teller machines, and other devices will replace the utilitarian check.

Banks introduced credit cards, first envisioned in 1887 by author Edward Bellamy as a replacement for cash, in the 1950s as a method of payment that substituted for checks. Franklin National Bank in Nassau County, New York pioneered the first bank-sponsored credit card in 1951.

The pressure to entice the American public to use credit cards over checks or currency is tremendous. In 1996, credit card companies mailed almost 2.5 billion unsolicited offers and organized millions of telephone solicitations to prospective customers. In recent years, these companies solicit each American an average of seven times a year for a new credit card.

It is estimated that 75% of American families have access to more than 460 million active credit cards in circulation and that Americans buy more than $300 billion in goods and services using credit cards. More than 70% of online transactions involve credit cards.

Lucrative profits have led banks to promote the use of credit cards over checks as a method of payment. From 1980 to 1996, the use of credit cards for personal consumption increased by 8%, while the use of checks for the same purpose increased by only 4%. In an interesting paradox, the single largest category of checks written by individuals is for payments to credit card accounts.

In 1996, nearly 19% of all U.S. purchases of goods and services were made by credit card, compared with 35% made by cash. Visa reported a rise of 18%, to $505 billion, in credit card transactions conducted in America for the twelve months through September 1997. The burger behemoth McDonald's announced in 2004 its plan to encourage credit card and debit card usage over cash in its 13,600 restaurants in the United States.

Currently, the average balance of a credit card account is about $600, and banks earn about $350 in interest alone for each account with a balance of $2,000. More revenue comes from transaction charges to merchants, which average between 2% and 4%. Cash-advance charges to customers add to the expanding revenue stream enjoyed by banks. One of the nation's largest credit card issuers, Citicorp in New York, has annual revenue of more than $4.5 billion in interest charges alone. Credit card advertising by banks also attracts new customers who open deposit accounts, borrow money, and employ other bank services.

Consumer experts argue that unrestrained use of credit cards pushes users into a quicksand of debt and contributes to the growing numbers of bankruptcies. In 1989, 40% of American families had credit card debt; more people owed money on their credit card purchases than on car loans or home mortgages. To give you an idea of the rate of escalation, consider this: In 1968, the amount of outstanding debt on U.S. credit cards approached $1 billion. By the end of 1996, this debt had grown to a stunning $238 billion, up 26% from $189 billion just two years earlier. In 2004, this debt had shot up to $785 billion. As part of this trend toward credit card debt, the number of delinquent card accounts in recent years has been growing at a rate of almost $2 per year.

As a method of bolstering profits and encouraging credit card use, major American companies, including Ford, AT&T, General Electric Credit, and the Gap, have teamed with banks to jointly sponsor credit cards. General Motors popularized these "co-branded credit cards" in 1992, but because of excessive operating costs and intense competition, their use in some sectors has precipitously declined. Within a year after its introduction, for instance, Pacific Bell cancelled its jointly sponsored credit card with Household Bank. But they are still pushed at many retailers, such as Macy's and Banana Republic.

Debit Cards

Debit cards function as electronic checks to automatically debit a bank account the moment a purchase is made. Check processing costs and the number of overdrafts are greatly reduced with debit cards, which has inspired such institutions as Bank of America and Chase to mass-mail debit cards to millions of households to spur their use. Beginning in the fall of 1997, MasterCard and Visa promoted debit card use for more than 70.5 million of their combined logo-bearing cardholders by limiting customer liability for unauthorized use to a $50 cap.

The number of authorized debit cardholders rose from 10 million in 1991 to 66.7 million in 1997, with purchases exceeding $62 billion. Unlike credit cards, debit card purchases are typically withdrawn immediately from a consumer's account.

Despite improvements in technology, credit and debit cards remain susceptible to fraud. Each year, issuers of credit cards lose about $1 billion from fraud, mostly from stolen credit cards. Banks lose another $3 billion from fraudulent bankruptcy filings. About 1.3 million credit card holders declared bankruptcy last year. However, the biggest losers are merchants, who absorb more than $10 billion each year from credit card–related fraud.

Banks prefer debit cards to credit cards because merchants are charged processing fees of up to 2%, and the long floats (the time between when the store gets paid for the sale and the credit card company gets paid by the consumer) that are common with credit card transactions are nonexistent. Debit cards are also hugely popular with students, many of whom cannot yet qualify for a credit card. In a pioneering attempt to reduce cash handling at major universities, Diebold created university-specific debit cards for on-campus transactions, nearly eliminating the need for cash. Students (or their parents) "fill up" the student card with money, and the student can then swipe it to pay for food, books, and even laundry.

Keypads & ATMs

The "In Touch" program sponsored by Seattle First National Bank in 1973 introduced the transfer of funds by telephone keypads. The program was discontinued in 1974 and sold to the Telephone Computing Service, Inc. To date, this method of fund transfer has not been widely used.

Vastly more successful were automated teller machines (ATMs), the electronic wonders that replaced checks for cash withdrawal. ATMs also allowed for fund transfers from one account to another and let consumers make deposits and loan payments. Chemical Bank in New York installed the first American ATM in New York City in 1969. Within 20 years, Bank of America operated the nation's largest bank-owned ATM network, with more than 6,800 machines.

By 2004, the number of ATMs operated by financial institutions and retail stores had surged to an estimated 1,150,000 worldwide, with a volume of transactions in the billions. NCR Corporation and Diebold are currently the world's leading suppliers of ATMs. Surveys show that half of all adult Americans use ATMs regularly.

Unlike checking accounts, which are managed by a large network of independent banks, control of ATMs is dominated by a limited number of banks. In California, for example, Bank of America, Wells Fargo Bank, and Chase control half of the ATMs. However, ATMs do not abolish the need for paper documentation. For every "checkless" transaction accomplished with an ATM, a paper receipt is generated for filing and reconciliation.

Although ATMs have traditionally been located on bank premises, this is expected to decline in the future. Already, over 41% of American ATMs are not located at banks. In California, Glendale Federal Bank has expanded its ATM network in McDonald's restaurants, United Artists theaters, and Kinko's copy centers; Chase ATMs are found inside CVS stores. ATMs are also appearing at convenience stores, shopping malls, airports, and almost every place where people spend money.

Skyrocketing fees have cast doubt about the cost-effectiveness of ATM transactions over checks for consumers. At this writing, 45% of the nation's ATMs assess surcharges of 25 cents to $2.50 per transaction. Consumers who use ATMs of banks other than their own pay additional "convenience fees." For many consumers, the cost-effectiveness of check writing far outweighs the "convenience" of electronic banking with ATMs. For banks, however, ATM transactions have a clear advantage; the average cost to a bank for a teller transaction is $1.07, but it's only 27 cents for an ATM transaction.

Although banks service the largest number of check redemptions, check-cashing businesses, first created in the 1940s, have proliferated across the United States in the last two decades. They're used by about 14% of American families without bank accounts. According to the Treasury Department, about 12 million American families can't afford to maintain regular bank accounts. There are an estimated 12,500 check-cashing stores in the United States, a number that is growing by 15 to 20% per year.

Check-cashing businesses are coming under increasing scrutiny and regulation. Beginning in January 1998, California imposed fines of up to $5,000 and six months in jail for proprietors of check-cashing establishments who operate without state permits.

Check-cashing stores are prevalent in low-income areas where people lack the resources to support and maintain bank accounts. In the poor area of South-Central Los Angeles, for example, check-cashing stores outnumber banks seven to one. Fees for cashing checks at these places range from an average of 2.34% for paychecks to an average of 9.36% for personal checks.

Supermarkets have also played a major role in checking transactions, redeeming about the same number of checks as banks.

Smart Cards

So-called "smart cards" were first introduced by Midland Bank in 1996 when a group of major banks, including Bank of America, Great Western, and Chase Manhattan, collaborated with a company called

Mondex; today Mondex cards are managed by MasterCard. These chip-embedded smart cards are treated exactly like cash, with transactions remaining relatively anonymous and fee-free (unlike with credit or debit cards). The consumer loads money onto a card and can use it anywhere it's accepted. The adoption of these cards has thus far been slow for a variety of reasons, including the limited number of places that accept it, the need to have a companion "smart wallet" to reload the card with funds, and the fact that if you lose a card loaded with money, you lose the money—it's just like cash.

Electronic Banking

By 2010, 205 million Americans used the internet with some regularity, and annual e-commerce retail sales had reached $173 billion—and was still growing fast. Furthermore, a remarkable 64% of American households paid at least some bills online.

Internet banks have recognized the potential for profitable opportunities and have begun to proliferate, offering services usually found at neighborhood banks with the added feature of expedient electronic communication.

Safety, privacy, and reliability for financial transactions are concerns that hold as much importance for today's internet user as it did for ancient Athenian merchants and traders. Sabotage of Fedwire or other major electronic transfer systems, computer viruses, and electrical power disturbances have the potential of causing economic calamity of catastrophic proportions.

With increasingly sophisticated electronic security measures for data communication, including encryption and electronic firewalls, the risk of intruder tampering has been minimized. Several methods of digital signature algorithms prevent data forgery and tampering. Utah recently became the first state to draft legislation recognizing digital signatures, and the American Bar Association created recommendations for the use of digital signatures in commerce.

However, experience has proven that electronic transfer systems are not infallible. On November 21, 1985, a new software program for the Bank of New York failed to properly reconcile checking balances with other banks, causing a massive shortage of funds. The computer error cost the bank $3.1 million in interest charges when it was forced to borrow $23 billion from the Federal Reserve to cover the shortage. Financial advisors have also warned consumers about the alarming rise of high-tech fraud directed at internet shoppers.

While storing data in digital form is highly efficient and dependable, it is far less durable than transactions recorded on quality paper. Recent studies have shown that magnetic tape, CD-ROMs, and other forms of electronic storage media have shorter life spans than originally believed. Archival paper may last hundreds of years, but digital data on various media will only last from 50 to 200 years. Also, the machines needed to read electronic data and software become obsolete even faster. Consequently, a tremendous expenditure of time and money may be necessary to maintain and update electronic financial records.

Electronic checks and online bill payment have shot up in popularity, as has the use of PayPal, which serves as an electronic intermediary for online commerce. Electronic checks and online bill payment significantly reduce operating costs associated with paper checks, since many of the manual steps are eliminated. For businesses this includes stuffing and opening envelopes, routing, reading, recording payment information, filing, sorting, creating deposit slips, and reconciliation of accounts. Bank handling expenses include encoding, filing, research, balancing, sorting, clearing, handling, and overall processing. In addition, electronic payments reduce expenses related to fraud associated with paper checks, such as forgery and check alteration.

With increasing payments for goods and services through electronic mechanisms, the volume of mail handled by the U.S. Postal Service has already been affected. Check writing indirectly supports the Postal Service; about half of the checks written by individuals are sent by mail. Electronic money transfers may also affect revenue generated from postal money orders, a method of payment especially important for people without checking accounts.

Banks, credit card companies, and manufacturers of electronic devices are developing handheld devices that process wireless mobile payments. Mobile payments by cellular telephone and other types of handheld devices are expected to reach $214 billion by 2015. Already, consumers can receive coupons on their cell phones through such websites as GoGoCoupons.com, and they can use their phones to check account balances and transfer funds.

Will Checks Survive?

As a consequence of increasing transactions via credit card, ATMs, and e-commerce, the supply of checks available for collectors will shrink. The recently enacted Check Clearing for the 21st Century Act will also influence the number of checks for collectors.

The Check Clearing for the 21st Century Act ("Check 21") created a new legal proof of payment, the "substitute check." Under Check 21, banks are no longer required to return the original written checks to their customers. Instead, they may provide a paper copy of the original check that the bank warrants as an accurate and legible representation of the original. The cost savings enjoyed by banks from the electronic processing allowed by Check 21 is estimated to be about $2 billion a year. However, because of this act, fewer checks will enter the pool for collectors.

Since their widespread adoption in the 18th century, checks have remained the dominant device for people to conduct financial transactions. Despite dire predictions from experts warning of their demise, they have withstood the test of time. Innovative computer technology has revolutionized check processing and the corresponding exchange of financial information. The universal success in check writing lies in its efficiency and simplicity. For these reasons, checks and check writing have survived electronic technology, and it seems quite likely that paper checks will continue their privileged status for many years to come.

However, if electronic methods of credit transfer, known as electronic data interchange (EDI), e-commerce, online bill payment, and electronic checks continue to grow in importance, those may well become the most common vehicles for conducting business and personal transactions. If that happens, checks in their current form will be used less often—and may even become obsolete. It is easy to see a future in which handwritten checks are deposed to the burgeoning list of collectible antiques, a reminder of a period of technology that includes mechanical typewriters, adding machines, and rubber endorsement stamps.

MODERN CHECK PROCESSING

With the establishment of the Federal Reserve System in 1913, bank identification numbers began to appear on checks. The earliest printed check with a bank identification number dates back to September 1, 1915. The first part of the hyphenated number refers to a specific city or state. Numbers 1 through 49 are reserved for cities; numbers 50 through 99 are reserved for each of the 50 states. Number 101 is used to identify U.S. territories and dependencies.

Two exceptions are the number 8000 and the transit routing number 0000. These routing numbers are used to identify traveler's checks and the Federal Reserve, respectively.

The second part of the hyphenated number usually identifies a bank in a specific state. For example, the number 1-1 refers to Bank of New York in New York State. At one time, separate numbers were used to identify specific branches of a bank. However, since the 1970s, only one number is used per bank, regardless of the number of branches. Many years ago, state treasuries and large corporations also had their own bank number printed on their checks.

With the passage of time, the hyphenated bank number was "fractionalized" with a denominator known as a transit routing number. The first two digits of the transit routing number correspond to one of the twelve Federal Reserve districts. The third digit usually refers to the Federal Reserve office within the preceding Fed district. The fourth digit usually indicates the state where the check is drawn.

After the advent of magnetic ink printing on checks in the 1950s, transit routing numbers were also printed in magnetic ink along the bottom left hand corner of checks. Transit routing numbers in this location are referred to as TR-ABA (Transit-American Bankers Association) numbers. Through an encoding system, the bank of first deposit adds magnetic numbers denoting the amount of the check.

Situated in between the TR-ABA number and the amount may be the preprinted account number and check number, also printed with magnetic ink. Reading and sorting machines read checks from right to left, starting with the amount field.

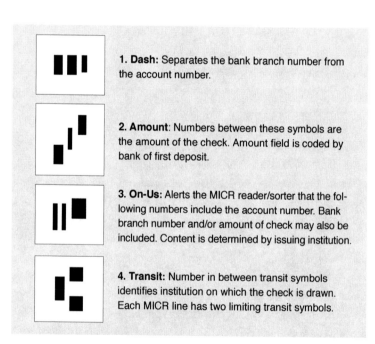

1. Dash: Separates the bank branch number from the account number.

2. Amount: Numbers between these symbols are the amount of the check. Amount field is coded by bank of first deposit.

3. On-Us: Alerts the MICR reader/sorter that the following numbers include the account number. Bank branch number and/or amount of check may also be included. Content is determined by issuing institution.

4. Transit: Number in between transit symbols identifies institution on which the check is drawn. Each MICR line has two limiting transit symbols.

The MICR line has four symbols for rapid check processing by magnetic scanning.

ERMA Symbols

The most common worldwide MICR encoding font is E-13B. The E-13B MICR font is used in Australia, Canada, Central America, Europe, the Far East, and the United States. Another MICR font, called the CMC-7, is used in Brazil, France, and some other European countries. The French computer company Machine Bull developed CMC-7. Unlike E-13B, MICR font CMC-7 has 26 alphabetic characters, one additional symbol, and different character dimensions. Finally, a few European countries use the optical fonts called OCR-A and OCR-B.

transit number   check number

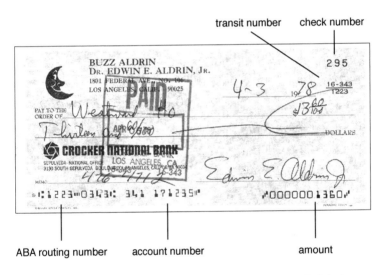

ABA routing number   account number   amount

MICR permits the high-speed processing of checks. A short, vertical dash-and-colon combination always borders both sides of the nine-digit ABA routing number (eight digits in the Buzz Aldrin check above, because it dates from 1978). This number is usually followed by the account number. The first bank receiving the check prints the amount drawn on the bottom right. At the upper right, below the check number, is the transit symbol, which is expressed as a fraction. The numerator is the ABA transit number, used to facilitate routing. Digits in the denominator correspond to branches of the Federal Reserve assigned to process checks from specific banks. The last digit in the denominator codes whether the check is acceptable for immediate or deferred credit. Logos and vignettes, like the moon above, are simply ornamental.

FAKES: FORGERIES & PROTECTION

Various security measures have developed over time to discourage check forgery. In the early days, check writers such as Francis E. Spinner, U.S. Treasury Secretary during the Civil War, devised a flourishing signature to discourage forgery. Many check writers also used elaborate paraphs (flourishes) below their signature. Some imprinted portraits of themselves on the front of checks to avoid misidentification and discourage fraud.

Such technical advances as the use of safety paper to expose erasures and alterations were incorporated into checks as early as the 1800s. Many types of security paper were chemically treated so that marks such as the word "void" become visible in areas of the check where erasers were used. Security paper also sometimes has repetitive backgrounds featuring logos and graphic images, which makes check alterations easier to detect.

Laser scanning techniques to improve the accuracy of check processing have evolved over the years to protect the check writer. However, despite these and other elaborate measures, check fraud remains a significant problem. Since 1966, more than 200 million fraudulent checks have been written for a face value of more than $4 billion. Annual losses from check fraud are estimated to be from $750 million to $1.5 billion.

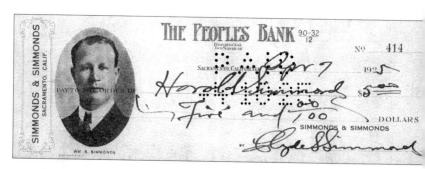

Portraits on checks provided rapid identification and discouraged fraudulent transactions. Portraits and engravings also served to advertise goods and services.

A check from Manhattan Bank in Kansas, with punch-out tabs to prevent alteration.

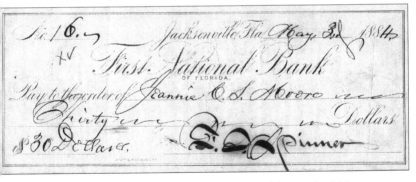

Treasury Secretary Francis E. Spinner developed an elaborate, flourishing signature to discourage forgery.

Since the inception of checks, criminals have figured out clever schemes to alter them. Early means to detect such alteration consisted of fine horizontal lines printed on the entry portion of checks. Erasures in these areas would deface the surface and produce permanent alterations that were easily spotted. In the 1800s, banks printed shaded areas on the handwritten entry portions of checks for the same reason, and some used punch holes to indicate the amount of a check.

Mechanical devices to prevent forgery began to appear in the 1870s. The earliest devices punched horizontal or circular holes in areas of the check that had written figures. In some cases, an embossed seal over the check amount was used to discourage alteration.

Check writing machines of increasingly sophisticated capabilities, using levers, tabs, keys, and other manipulating mechanisms, began to appear after the Civil War. Numerical figures on checks were either embossed, printed, or hole punched.

Check Fraud Protection

The earliest check writers were concerned with fraud, and for good reason—criminals became adept at altering payor names, check amounts, and other written additions to printed checks. The creativity of check designers to prevent fraud is an interesting and educational facet of check collecting that has evolved with advancing technology.

Designers developed a variety of security printing techniques. Early check-protection features included printing very fine and closely aligned lines in the written areas to make alterations more conspicuous. Embossed dots were also used for this purpose. Checks were also printed with tabs for check amounts as a means to confirm the amounts written on the checks.

To prevent high-level fraud, banks often printed a financial limit on the face of the check. Perforated cancellations were used to discourage alteration of numbers and written text. Today, checks printed with the many methods to discourage fraud appeal to a specialized group of collectors.

Book No. 40 6 10
Page 311 8

Auburn, N. Y. July 27 1898

AUBURN SAVINGS BANK,

ESTABLISHED 1849.

Pay to L. P. Becker .... or Bearer,

One hundred five **Dollars,**

$ 105.00   Mary A. Becker

is Check will not be paid unless accompanied by the Pass Book.

The imprint notice "This Check will not be paid unless accompanied by the Pass Book" helped bankers identify the person cashing a check."

Mechanical printing devices, also known as check protectors, were devised to discourage check alteration and prevent fraud. Max Emanuel Berolzheimer of New York City is credited with the first United States patent for a check-protecting device. Although his patent was issued in 1869, there is no evidence that his device was ever actually manufactured.

Check protectors were able to emboss paper where figures were written, punch out amounts with small perforations, imprint Arabic numerals and English words, insert indelible ink on paper, or print monetary limits on checks so that upper limits were denoted.

At least twenty companies manufactured check-protecting devices starting in the early 1800s. Some of the most recognizable companies included Hedman (Chicago, Illinois), Paymaster (Chicago, Illinois), Safe-Guard (Seguin, Texas), and G.W. Todd (Rochester, New York).

Manual imprinters, like this Hedman check writer, were popular from the 1920s through 1960s.

A great number of these check-protecting devices still exist and are avidly sought by collectors of checks and antique office equipment.

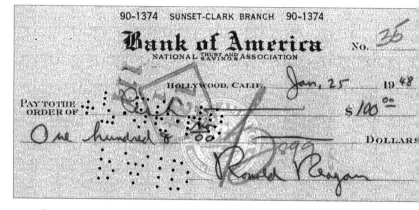

Ronald Reagan's check for cash was cancelled with a crayon "B" handwritten across his signature.

Imprints from mechanical check writers clearly specified amounts, so the checks couldn't be easily altered.

CHECK CANCELLATIONS

Cancellation marks on a check show that the bank actually paid the funds to the payee. A cancellation of a check voids the pay order so the check cannot be reprocessed. Some cancellation marks may be visible on the front (recto) of a check. Others have endorsement and routing numbers imprinted on the back (verso). Both types signify transfer of funds by the bank.

Hand Alterations

The most common early form of cancellation was to simply cross out the signature of the maker. In many instances, bank employees handwrote "Paid" or "X" in a vertical orientation in the center of a check. Handwritten notations including date and name were sometimes included. Early American checks often had segments that included the signature torn off the check to denote that payment had been made.

Mechanical

Cuts, with or without paper loss, were used on checks as early as the late 1700s. A design such as a V, Y, or X was cut into the check. Later, in the 1870s, punch hole cancellations in a multitude of designs and patterns appeared. Some had round holes while others had, for example, diamond configurations. Embossing of checks with notations such as "Paid" or the name of the bank were used in the 1850s and 1860s. Finally, checks were often cancelled by hand with rubber stamps or by machines.

BANK SIGNATURE CARDS

Banks retain signature cards on file as a reliable record of ownership and title to an account. They often use these cards to confirming signatures and the background information of their customers. Signatures on these cards are virtually always authentic examples. For autograph collectors, these cards are a dream come true. Many autograph check collectors will acquire a signature card when an autographed check from a particular personality is not available.

Howard Hughes's authentic bank signature card. The card is stamped "signature verified," and the background information printed on the card provides correlative facts about Hughes.

The Basics of Check Collecting

The popular avocation of check collecting consists of acquiring and preserving checks. The collector is, in a real sense, a guardian of human history, since so much of modern civilization is represented in its financial instruments, notably checks.

THE LEGAL DEFINITION

A modern check is legally defined in Section 3-104 of the Uniform Commercial Code (UCC) as a negotiable instrument having three components:

· The signature of the maker (drawer).
· A specified sum of money to the order of the payee.
· Be drawn on a bank and payable on demand.

Modern checks have preprinted numbers of the face of the check. These numbers provide essential financial information: bank numbers, routing numbers, check numbers, and identification numbers of one type or another. Manuscript checks, also known as holographic checks, are completely handwritten. Manuscript checks are entirely legal but may not be accepted by a bank because of concerns about authenticity.

THEMES & CATEGORIES

The collecting themes of checks are as varied as their subject matters. Some of the most popular themes include celebrity-autographed checks, revenue-stamped checks, and checks with interesting vignettes.

Pray pay to Dr Fauquier the three per cent Dividend due
at Midsummer last upon twenty & one thousand six hundred
& ninety six pounds six shillings & four pence south sea stock
I am entituled unto in the Companies books; & his receipt
shall be your sufficient Discharge from

8 Aug. 1722.

To the Accomptant
of the South Sea
Company.

Yor humble servant
Isaac Newton

20/1

A manuscript check written by Isaac Newton. This check is particularly note-
worthy because it connects Newton with the infamous South Sea Company.
Photo: Scott J. Winslow

Collectors have sought celebrity-autographed checks that have existed since the beginning of America. This is why autographed checks from illustrious individuals, including Thomas Jefferson and George Washington, are still in existence; they have been passed on from one generation of collectors to another.

Collecting checks with revenue stamps has experienced surging popularity. Checks with revenue stamps appeal to philatelists (stamp collectors), historians, and those who treasure engraved stamp images for their intrinsic beauty.

Many of the checks manufactured in the 1800s and 1900s were adorned with beautiful vignettes. Checks with vignettes constitute one of the most fascinating areas of check collecting. Images of Native Americans, presidents, cities, states, geologic formations, railroads, and agriculture are among thousands of themes available for check collectors. Historical mining scenes on checks from California, Colorado, Idaho, Montana, and Nevada appeal to a great number of collectors. Similarly, many collectors avidly seek checks associated with specific banks. Many of these exquisite vignettes have an extremely high level of artistic detail and technical excellence. They help us appreciate the art of engraving and design.

The key point for check collectors is selecting an appealing category. By investing in an area that appeals to your personal taste, there will always be pleasure in owning a collection that you have built from the ground up. If your collection increases in value, then consider it an incidental benefit.

With so many kinds of checks available, you will inevitably find an area you find captivating. Studying the background and details of your growing collection will provide a fascinating educational experience.

Examples of Check Collecting Categories

A great many niches occupy the world of check collecting, each with its own appeal for individual collectors. Some prefer checks with elaborately engraved vignettes. Others appreciate any form of check with an authentic signature from a famous individual. Checks bearing revenue stamps are attractive to many check and stamp collectors.

Examples of check collecting categories include:

Allegorical themes	Fonts
Bank specific	Government
Black history	High monetary amounts
Blind handicap	Internal Revenue Service
Bounced	Logos
Business	Old West
Cancellations	Payroll
Celebrity	Portraits
Celebrity autographed	Refund/rebate
Commemorative	Regional
City specific	Revenue stamped
Civil War	Revolutionary War
Coca-Cola	Safety & security
Company specific	Season's greetings
Content	Sports
Counter	Travelers
Country specific	Vignettes
Emergency scrip	Wells Fargo
Errors & omissions	
Forgeries	

CELEBRITY CHECKS

Recent years have seen an upswing in collecting checks signed by interesting notables. Their popularity resides in the relative ease of obtaining autographed checks and the fact that cancelled checks have a high degree of authenticity. Many autograph collectors who collected autographs on photographs, album pages, or index cards were disappointed to discover that many of these items were signed by a

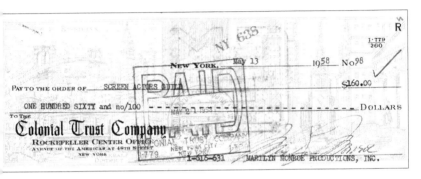

Among the most readily accessible and yet most expensive modern celebrity checks available for collectors are ones signed by Marilyn Monroe. This one has an interesting association—it is addressed to the Screen Actors Guild and signed by Monroe.

A Season's Greetings check signed by Bob's Big Boy restaurant founder Robert Wian. Wian made the first double-decker hamburger.

mechanical device, rubber stamp, or secretarial assistant.

Jean Harlow's mother, for example, forged her famous daughter's signature on glamour photos to satisfy the requests of numerous autograph collectors. Frank Sinatra's secretaries signed many of his "personally inscribed" photos for swarms of adoring fans. Many celebrities simply do not have the time to supply a large number of fans with signatures on photos, magazines, or album pages.

Instead, many autograph collectors have gravitated to cancelled checks as an accessible and reliable means of autograph collecting. The signatures of famous people on checks have become the primary focus for many collectors.

However, although most checks have original signatures, one must beware of printed or rubber-stamped facsimile signatures.

NOTE:
Be cautious when purchasing checks from modern celebrities when they first appear. Hordes of their checks may flood the market, resulting in lower prices.

REVENUE STAMPS ON CHECKS

The American Civil War imposed a tremendous burden on the United States Treasury. At first, Treasury Secretary Salmon Chase anticipated a short and economically inconsequential conflict. However, it soon became apparent that the war would evolve into a prolonged and expensive undertaking. Up until the time of the Civil War, the primary source of revenue for the federal government was customs duties, which raised less than $40 million. Income from individual states to the United States Treasury by the first Civil War tax, which was enacted on August 5, 1861, was woefully inadequate. The government needed a radical method of generating income for the North.

Orange revenue stamps were the first adhesive revenue stamps produced in America. Checks with embossed revenue stamps were used in the 1700s. This check with an affixed revenue stamp is signed by an attorney who administered the famous Amnesty Oath to Civil War general Robert E. Lee.

Soon came laws to tax all sorts of items, including liquor, playing cards, medicines, perfumes, and virtually every transaction involving personal property. Checks were among those taxable items. The war cost the federal government approximately $3 billion. Revenue stamps, including those used with checks, brought $340 million into the coffers of the U.S. Treasury. Implementing a wide variety of taxes provided a steady flow of income that bolstered the government's credibility in the bond market. From their inception in 1862 through 1883, more than nine billion revenue stamps were produced for the benefit of the federal government. About one billion of these stamps were for bank checks.

In contrast, the Confederacy did not issue revenue stamps to raise money for the war. Instead, the Confederate government relied primarily on loans and non-interest-bearing notes. Revenue from taxes provided only 8% of the Confederate government's funding. Failure to raise sufficient funds limited the ability of the Confederacy to fight the Civil War.

Unlike postage stamps, which represent a fee paid for the service of delivering a piece of mail, revenue stamps are used to document a tax payment. Federal, state, provincial, and municipal governments in many countries have used revenue stamps on checks to raise money. Revenue stamps are often affixed to fiscal documents, including checks and stock certificates. The *Scott Specialized Catalogue of*

United States Stamps and Covers has categorized these issues. The identifying numbers appearing in this book refer to Scott's catalogue classification.

The use of stamps for collecting tax revenue appears to have been invented by the Dutch in 1624. They were first used in England in 1694 by order of an act that was passed to raise money for the war with France. In 1797, the British introduced the stamp tax in India to raise revenue for the East India Company.

The need to raise funds for the federal government during the American Civil War led to the Revenue Stamp Act of July 1, 1862, which established the Internal Revenue Service and mandated the use of revenue stamps. The new law stipulated that bank checks, drafts, and pay orders with a value greater than $20 and not exceeding $100 must bear an affixed revenue stamp as evidence of a tax payment. This law took effect on October 1, 1862.

Financial documents without revenue stamps were not accepted as negotiable instruments or admissible as evidence in legal matters. Failure to apply an adhesive revenue stamp to a check was subject to a fine of $50. The only exemptions to this requirement were financial documents issued by a federal, state, or municipal government. For instance, the Asylum for the Chronic Insane, an institution established by the Massachusetts state legislature, had "No Stamp Required" printed on their checks as a reminder of their tax-exempt status.

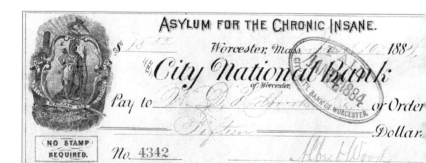

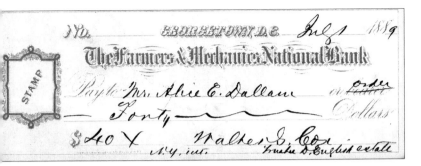

Stewart Warren & Co. in New York City printed checks with a box for affixing revenue stamps.

The Three Issues of Revenue Stamps

The government commissioned three issues of adhesive revenue stamps. The first ran from 1862 to 1871 and was produced by the engraving and printing firm of Butler and Carpenter of Philadelphia. They delivered their two-cent orange revenue stamps to the Treasury Department on September 29, 1862.

First-issue revenue stamps were imperforate (no line of border holes), part perforate (lines of holes on opposite borders), or completely perforate (holes on all four sides). Paper for the revenue stamp consisted of textured wove without watermark identification. From September 1862 through September 1871, revenue stamps for bank checks consisted of thick paper. During this time, printers increasingly used silk fibers in the stamp paper.

In October 1862, the color of the two-cent revenue stamp was changed from orange to blue. This change drew sharp criticism, because ink cancellations were not as easily discerned. In August 1865, the color of the two-cent revenue stamp was changed back to orange. All the other denominations retained their original colors.

Second-issue revenue stamps arrived in 1871 but were quickly replaced by a third issue, which had different colors for six denominations. Two-cent and five-cent issues, which were most often used on checks and promissory notes, were printed in orange and black. Blue adhesive revenue stamps were produced from 1875 through 1878.

Forgeries

Curiously, counterfeiting of revenue stamps was never a major problem, probably because of the high investment and expertise needed to produce good forgeries. However, the government was concerned about losing revenue when people washed the cancellations off revenue stamps so they could be reused.

To discourage this washing, second and third issues of affixable revenue stamps were printed on "chameleon paper." Patented by James M. Wilcox of Glen Mills, Pennsylvania, chameleon paper was designed to foil attempts to remove cancellations with acid and alkali bleaches. Chameleon paper contained silk fibers impregnated with red and blue dye that were sensitized by a chemical treatment. Any attempt to bleach out a cancellation caused the discharge of the dye and discoloration of the stamp.

A New Law & New Way of Printing Checks

A new revenue law that became effective in August of 1864 required a two-cent tax on all bank checks and drafts payable on sight, regardless of the amount of the transaction. No longer could a check writer avoid the tax by paying a large debt with multiple checks, each for less than the $20 minimum. As a result, it became common to print revenue stamps directly onto checks and drafts.

The American Phototype Company of New York earned the first contract for printing revenue imprints on documents in May of 1865. American Phototype was the principal supplier of revenue-imprinted checks, producing more than half of the supply. It developed six types of revenue-imprinted checks, including ones with images of an eagle and George Washington. Its final design was a two-cent imprinted stamp featuring a facial profile of Ben Franklin.

Before this new law, check printers often included a plain or ornate box on their checks to mark where to place revenue stamps. When printers started imprinting revenue stamps right onto checks, the check was not necessarily redesigned, and the superfluous stamp box often remained.

From at least May of 1868, the Carpenter Company in Philadelphia also produced two-cent revenue imprints. Its designs were similar to those of its adhesive stamps. Its final design, approved in 1874, featured a bust profile of George Washington that was available in eight colors.

With few exceptions, one printer produced a check, and a second printer imprinted the actual revenue stamp. A rare example exists of a check and Type N imprinted revenue stamp produced by one printer, Alexander Trochsler & Company of Boston. This firm was authorized to produce revenue-imprinted checks in mid-1873.

A short time later, in the fall of 1874, the firm of Morey and Sherwood in Chicago produced revenue imprints on bank checks (Scott Type RN-0). Its imprints consisted of the head of Liberty flanked by the opposite faces of a two-cent coin. Cancelled checks from banks bearing this extremely rare revenue imprint are dated 1875 and have been identified in banks from Illinois, Iowa, Missouri, and Wisconsin. Cancelled checks with the Scott Type RN-0 imprint have been sold at auction for considerable sums, since fewer than 100 examples are known to exist.

In 1875, the Graphic Company of New York began producing the Type RN-G imprints on checks. This orange revenue imprint shows Liberty in a diamond-shape frame. This imprint enjoyed widespread use from 1875 until 1883 and is considered the most commonly available Civil War imprinted revenue stamp on a check.

Printers used four different two-cent adhesive stamps on financial documents, including bank checks (Scott Type R), and fifteen types of two-cent imprints for similar items (Scott Type RN). The situation was more complicated with promissory notes; the amount of stamp tax on promissory notes and foreign exchange bills depended on the amount of the transaction.

Of particular interest for signature collectors is that whenever an adhesive stamp was used, the person using the financial document (say, the check writer) was required to write or imprint in ink his initials and the date in a distinct and legible manner. This form of cancellation prevented the stamp from being used repeatedly. Although not rigidly enforced, failure to adequately cancel a revenue stamp was subject to a $50 penalty. As a result, many collectible financial documents signed by noteworthy figures also bear their initials.

When the government contract with Joseph R. Carpenter for printing revenue stamps expired on August 31, 1875, the National Bank Note Company of New York held the contract through early 1879. It prepared new designs for the two-cent revenue stamp that were mandated by the bank check tax. In October of 1880, the Bureau of Engraving and Printing took over printing all revenue stamps.

Finally, on July 1, 1883, the federal government abolished all documentary and proprietary revenue-stamp taxes, including taxes on checks. From their inception in 1862 through 1883, more than nine billion revenue stamps were produced for the benefit of the federal government. About one billion of these stamps were for bank checks. The majority of bank checks used for tax revenue were of the imprinted variety.

Owners of unused imprinted checks were offered a limited time to remit their checks for a tax refund. These redeemed checks were stamped "stamp redeemed" in a violet color and returned to the purchaser for later use. This redemption notice was usually stamped so

Federal, state, provincial, and municipal governments in many countries have used revenue stamps on checks. This example shows a Canadian stamp that helped finance the nation's expenses in World War I.

that it read upward, but many examples may be found where it reads downward or horizontally.

State Revenue Stamps

Beginning in 1865 and continuing through the 1870s, Nevada was the only state in the U.S. to imprint its own revenue stamps on checks. Nevada checks bore a variety of stamp colors, including orange, green, and violet. The famous "Purple Nevada" check consists of a violet Nevada revenue stamp imprinted on a check that bears a federal imprinted revenue stamp.

Great Depression Check Tax

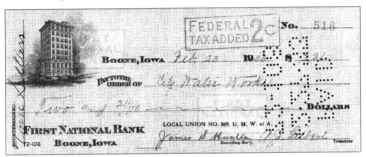

Checks written from 1932 to 1935 were assessed two cents by the U.S. Government. Checks processed for this tax payment bore a rubber-stamp notice.

United States Government Assessment on Bank Checks

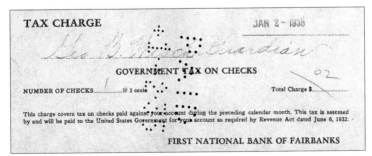

Check writers during the Great Depression received statements notifying them of their tax assessment on bank checks.

Revenue Stamps Return

The U.S. Government looked to adhesive revenue stamps again in 1898, to help finance the Spanish-American War. Most checks payable were taxed from July 1, 1898 through June 30, 1901, when the tax act was repealed. Checks with revenue stamps that were redeemed for credit after the Spanish-American War were punched with small, round holes.

The use of adhesive stamps on checks to raise money for the federal government was resurrected once again during World War I.

The United States was again challenged with dire financial difficulties during the Great Depression of the 1930s. The Revenue Act of 1932 attempted to rescue the American economy from the depths of the Depression. This legislation, signed into law by President Herbert Hoover on June 6, 1932, tried to balance the federal budget by dramatically raising income taxes, increasing postal rates, doubling estate taxes, imposing excise taxes, taxing gasoline for the first time, and taxing bank checks. Effective June 21, 1932, a two-cent tax was levied on each check, draft, and pay order.

This time, a two-cent tax on checks was simply withdrawn from a check writer's bank account for each check that was processed by the bank. Instead of revenue stamps, banks used a variety of rubber stamps with a two-cent withdrawal notification. Checks were commonly stamped "U.S. Tax 2c." Check writers also received account slips that showed amounts levied by the government against their accounts. This program did not last long – the Revenue Act of 1934 terminated the tax on December 31, 1934. Checks with a two-cent revenue imprint were occasionally submitted for processing after legal termination of tax on bank checks. These revenue-imprinted checks were not subject to a levy on the check writers account.

The fascinating association between revenue stamps and checks has become a subject of intense interest to philatelists, notaphilists, scripophilists, legal historians, economists, and autograph buffs. Revenue stamps on checks have also steadily gained in popularity over the past decade.

REVENUE-IMPRINT FACSIMILES

After the two-cent revenue stamp was discontinued in 1883, designs that resembled the revenue imprint continued to appear on checks. These designs were strictly ornamental, enhancing the appearance of checks and making them appear genuine. These revenue-imprint facsimiles are referred to in stamp catalogues as RN-FAC.

John D. Rockefeller's check to B. Altman and Company bears an imprint facsimile with his famous initials.

Revenue Stamps: A Civil War–Era Timeline

November 1860: Abraham Lincoln elected President of the United States.

April 12, 1861: Onset of military action marks the start of the American Civil War when Confederate forces fire on Fort Sumter in Charleston Harbor, South Carolina.

July 21, 1861: First major battle of the Civil War at Henry Hill, Virginia Manassas Battlefield. Nearly 900 soldiers and one civilian are killed.

July 1, 1862: President Lincoln signs the Revenue Act, creating the first federal income tax. The office of Commissioner of Internal Revenue is established within the Treasury Department. Bank checks for $20 or more are taxed with a two-cent revenue tax. Postmasters, stationers, national banks, and authorized tax collectors are among the list of vendors authorized to sell revenue stamps. The penalty for counterfeiting or defrauding the Treasury is a fine not to exceed $1,000 and up to five years of imprisonment or confinement to hard labor. The person affixing a revenue stamp is required to write his initials and date on the stamp so it cannot be used again, or be subject to a $50 fine. A person making payment by domestic check or accepting payment by domestic check without a proper revenue stamp is subject to a $200 fine and invalidation of the document. Similar infractions originating from a foreign bank check are subject to a $100 fine.

July 16, 1862: George Boutwell becomes the first Commissioner of Internal Revenue, a job he holds until March of 1863.

August 8, 1862: The United States Treasury accepts bids to produce revenue stamps. The Philadelphia firm of Butler & Carpenter is awarded the contract. John Butler is an engraver and printer as well as a close friend of Abraham Lincoln. Joseph Carpenter is the son of Samuel Carpenter, an engraver and partner in Toppan, Carpenter Co., which produced postal stamps for the U.S. Government in 1851 and 1857. (In 1857, the firm Toppan, Carpenter Co. produced the first perforated stamp sheets in America.) Its one-year contract begins October 1, 1862. Butler & Carpenter are paid thirteen cents for each thousand stamps produced. In 1863, their rate of reimbursement climbs to 33 cents for each thousand stamps. The company charges the U.S. Government $19,000 for 106 engraved plates for printing revenue stamps.

September 17, 1862: Production of orange two-cent revenue stamps for bank checks begins.

September 27, 1862: First revenue stamps issued by Butler & Carpenter are delivered to the U.S. Treasury. These two-cent adhesive bank stamps are orange and do not have a watermark. The two-cent orange bank stamps are produced in both perforated and part-perforate varities.

October 1, 1862: Taxpayers are required to match a specific stamp with a type of document. This is the start of the obligatory matching use (OMU) period. However, only bank check revenue stamps are available to the public. Checks with revenue stamps from October 1862 are rare and highly coveted by collectors. Government documents are exempt from the stamp tax.

October 10, 1862: Two-cent bank stamps are printed in blue until August 10, 1864.

November 1862: Butler & Carpenter include "unfinished" non-perforated and partially perforated revenue stamps to expediently meet high demand.

December 25, 1862: Taxpayers are no longer required to match stamps with documents. Taxpayers are also required to cancel revenue stamps with their initials and date of usage.

March 18, 1863: Joseph Lewis appointed second Commissioner of Internal Revenue.

June 30, 1864: Revenue law removes the $20 threshold for taxing checks, so checks of all amounts are now taxed. This stops the practice of writing multiple checks for less than $20 to pay for larger debts, to avoid the tax on checks of $20 or more. The Revenue Tax Act of 1864 takes effect August 1, 1865.

June 1865: The first bank checks bearing imprinted revenue stamps are produced.

August 3, 1865: American Phototype Company of New York imprints revenue stamps on paper. The earliest existing revenue-stamped check is dated August 3, 1865 and is drawn on the American Exchange Bank of New York. The two-cent imprint is located along the left margin of the check and consists of a rectangular vignette of an eagle standing with raised wings in an oval frame. The earliest revenue-stamped check has red stamps, but a variety of colors are produced, with orange being the most common color. Revenue stamps are also imprinted in various locations on a check, with the center being the most common location.

April 12, 1865: Confederate leader Robert E. Lee surrenders to Ulysses S. Grant at Appomattox, Virginia, and the Civil War formally ends. More than 625,000 soldiers died during the war, almost equal to the military toll in the Revolutionary War, World War I, World War II, Korea, and Vietnam combined.

June 1866: The firm of Butler & Carpenter produces revenue-stamped paper to be used in printing checks.

October 1868: John Butler dies. The firm continues as Carpenter Co.

March 12, 1869: George Boutwell appointed Secretary of the United States Treasury.

1872: Taxes on all document stamps except the two-cent bank check are eliminated.

1875: Carpenter loses the revenue-stamp contract to National Bank Note Company.

1878: American Bank Note Company is awarded the revenue-stamp contract.

1881: The Bureau of Engraving and Printing receives the revenue-stamp contract.

July 1, 1883: Internal revenue (income tax) is repealed, including the revenue-stamp requirement on bank checks.

1884: Stamp dealer E. B. Sterling purchases the archive of Butler & Carpenter Co. from Joseph Carpenter.

June 28, 1898: Tax Act passes to finance Spanish-American War. Revenue stamps once again generate income for the U.S. Treasury.

LOGOS & VIGNETTES

Craftsmen who had become proficient at designing and printing American currency also applied their talents to check design. Many ornate and beautiful vignettes portraying allegorical figures were applied to checks. The number of subjects and scope of vignettes used to adorn checks are virtually unlimited.

Vignettes included personifications of such subjects as Liberty, Freedom, Agriculture, Industry, Navigation, Commerce, Peace, Medicine, and Justice. These allegorical figures and symbols were used to attract customers to a particular bank and to discourage counterfeiting.

Modern checks are often printed with background illustrations that include sports, pets, pastoral settings, cartoon characters, circus themes, flowers, Americana, waterscapes, and whimsical themes.

Logos

Many companies and businesses apply their logos to checks as a form of branding and as a symbol of strength and permanency.

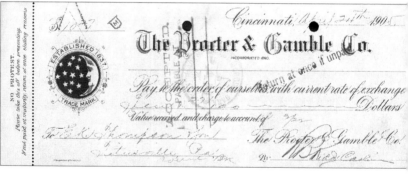

Created in 1851 by Mr. Procter and Mr. Gamble, this controversial logo signifying the stars and the moon was placed on crates of Star candles and on some checks. The trademark was registered with the U.S. Patent Office in 1882. But in the 1890s, rumors that the logo represented Satanism forced the company to discontinue its use.

Images of geologic formations on checks identify the location of a bank and add visual appeal. In this case, Whitewood Banking Company used the image of Devil's Tower in the Black Hills of South Dakota to connote power and prestige.

Geologic Formations

Many banks and businesses include images of recognizable geologic landmarks on their checks, and sometimes images of landmarks are used as logos. Repeated public exposure to these images on checks and other documents became a useful marketing tool. Some businesses have trademarked the geologic images they have used on checks.

Examples of Vignettes

Vignettes on checks are decorative illustrations usually present along a check's upper or left margin. A vignette may be a simple sketch, lithograph, photograph, cartoon illustration, or detailed engraving. These vignettes may be made by high-production printing presses or from an engraving that has been painstakingly fashioned by skilled engravers.

The technique of engraving, known since at least 1446, involves the creation of incisions in wood or metal using specialized tools. The craftsman applies ink to the engraved plate and carefully wipes it so only the ink is contained within the engraved lines. He then presses slightly dampened paper onto the plate to create an inked impression on the paper. Many collectors specialize in checks bearing engraved vignettes, attracted by the creative artwork by expert engravers.

Vignettes include:

Abraham Lincoln
Allegorical
America

Anchors
Angels
Animals
Arm & Hammer
Bank buildings
Bears
Beehives
Ben Franklin
Birds
Blacksmiths
Blind institutions
Boats
Breweries
Bridges
Buildings
Canals
Cattle

Children
Cigars
Coal
Coca-Cola
Coffee
Commerce
Cookware
Cotton
Cows
Country
Crowns
Deer
Divers
Dogs
Dog and safe
Dragons
Druggists
Ducks
Eagles
Eagle & flag
Eagle & shield
Eagle on globe

Education
Elk
Engravings
Farm animals
Farmers
Farming

Fire engines
Fire insurance
Firemen
Fish
Flags
Flowers
Forts
Furniture
Geologic formations

DEVILS TOWER, BLACK HILLS
615 FEET HIGH

George Washington

Girls

Globe

Hope

Horses

Indians

Indian Territories

Ino & Bacchus

Insufficient funds

Insurance

Justice

Keystone

Ladies

Leatherstocking

Liberty

Lighthouses

Lions

Log cabins

Lumber

Machinists

Men

Match & medicine

Miners

Mining

Misprints

Monograms

Mormonism

Negroes

Oil

Otters

Payroll

Patent machine

Portraits

Private die

Pyramids

Railroads

Refund/rebates

Regional

Revenue stamps

Rifles

Safes

Sailors

Sailing ship

Samples

Scales

Sea serpents

Season's greetings

Security printing

Sheep

Shields

Ships

Shoes

Soldiers

Specimen checks

Spices

State seals

Steamboats

Steamships

Tea

Telegraph lines

Territorial

Thomas Jefferson

Tobacco

Tom Thumb

Tools

Trains

Transportation

Travelers

Umbrellas

U.S. Government

Wagon trains

Wells Fargo

Wine

Women

FAMOUS BANKS

Banks of historic significance are appealing to many check collectors. Certain banks may be interesting because of their longevity, association with notable individuals, or contribution to economic development. The Bank of England, Bank of America, and Wells Fargo Bank are three notable examples of historically important banks for collectors.

Bank of England

The Bank of England sometimes referred to as "The Old Lady of Threadneedle Street," was founded in 1694. Its most famous Chief Cashier was Abraham Newland, who served the bank from 1778 through 1807. From 1782 until 1807, currency from the Bank of England was known as "Newlands,'" because Abraham Newland's name appeared in the promissory clause.

Bank of America

A.P. Giannini founded the Bank of Italy in San Francisco in 1904. In 1909, he opened the first branch in San Jose and expanded his business to become the first transcontinental banking network in America. In 1930 he changed the name to Bank of America. By 1949, it was the largest bank in the world, with 522 branches. After acquiring FleetBoston Bank in 2004, Bank of America had 5,700 branches.

Wells Fargo Bank

Wells Fargo Bank has appeal for many check collectors because of its famous history and the role it played in the Old West. Many individuals living today can remember having relatives who worked for Wells Fargo as stage drivers, tellers, and security officers. Autographs by Henry Wells and William Fargo are quite common on stock certificates but very uncommon on checks.

Recorded 12. April 1780

Recd the 14 April 1780 Of the Right Honble Philip Earl of Hardwicke one of the Four Tellers of his Majesty's Receipt of Exchequer the Sum of One Hundred & Three Thousand One Hundred & Twenty nine Pounds Eight Shillings & one halfpenny in part of an Order for £385,065.17.11¼ Dated the 5 April 1780 & payable to the Chief Cashier &c of the Govr & Comp. of the Bank of England

Newland

I say Recd by me

£103,129.8.½

Witness

A Cowper

In the document above, Abraham Newland (1730-1807) signs a receipt as Chief Cashier for the Bank of England.

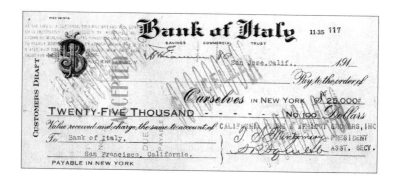

In 1909, A.P. Giannini opened the Bank of Italy in San Jose, California. It was the first branch outside of his home bank in San Francisco and the beginning of an empire that became Bank of America, the world's largest and wealthiest privately held banking institution. A.P. Giannini signed his approval of the customer draft at the top of this page beneath the Bank of Italy imprint.

Founded in 1852, Wells Fargo is now the fifth largest bank in the United States. This check is signed by Wells Fargo's first president, Edwin Morgan (left). He was also noted for his role in the founding of American Express.

BANK COLLECTING THEMES

Some collectors seek examples from a particular theme, and the number of themes is almost countless. Banking themes of interest to check collectors include:

First black-owned banks in America (1888)

· Savings Bank of the Grand Fountain United Order of the Reformers in Richmond, Virginia.
· Capital Savings Bank of Washington, D.C.

First bank to implement bank-sponsored credit cards (1952)

· Franklin National Bank of Long Island, Franklin Square, New York

First bank to utilize internet banking (1995)

· Security First Network Bank

First bank in Los Angeles (1868)

· Alvin, Hayward & Co.

First British joint stock bank (1826)

· Lancaster Banking Company

Bank of the British Royalty for over 200 years

· Coutts & Co.

First bank with over $1 trillion in assets

· Citigroup, Inc., founded in 1901

Bank with the most customers

· Citigroup, Inc., with about 200 million customers in more than 100 countries

Oldest continually operating bank in America

· Bank of New York, which began operations on February 23, 1784

Babe Ruth's bank

· Chemical Bank of New York

First bank in America

· Bank of North America

First bank in New York City

· Bank of New York; organized by Alexander Hamilton

Largest African-American-owned bank in the United States
- Carver Federal Savings Bank; chartered in New York in 1984

First bank in California
- Naglee & Stinton; opened January 9, 1849

First bank in Pasadena, California
- First National (started as Pasadena Bank); incorporated in December of 1884

European bank founded by Meyer Amschel Rothschild
- Reichsbank of Germany

Bank started by the "Bonanza Kings' of the Comstock Lode
- Nevada Bank in 1875; started in California

First safe deposit system in San Francisco
- California Safe Deposit Company in 1875

Bank founded by one of the "Big Four" transcontinental railroad entrepreneurs
- Crocker National Bank; founded in 1883 by William H. Crocker, grandson of railroader Charles Crocker

BLACK HISTORY

Many collectors specialize in checks associated with the history of Negro slavery and black history. Checks originating from the Southern states often featured images of black figures or depictions of life for black fieldworkers. In this check, for example, the interesting vignette shows black cotton pickers on a Georgia bank check.

COMPANY CHECKS

Some collectors seek checks issued by or depicting certain firms. Company checks may represent historic phases in the history of a company.

Coca-Cola and Pepsi-Cola have nostalgic value for many check collectors. In particular, checks from Coca-Cola's various bottling companies have a dedicated following.

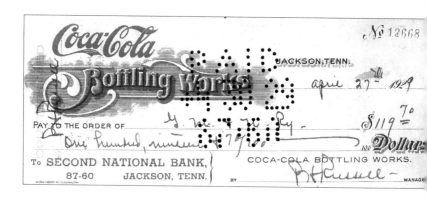

Baseball legend Ty Cobb used some of his fortune to invest in Coca-Cola bottling plants.

CONTENT ASSOCIATION CHECKS

A check with interesting or meaningful attributes is described as having significant content. For example, a check written on a date that connects the check writer to an important date may have an interesting association. Checks that reveal the personal preferences, character, or previously unknown aspect of the check writer's life are especially desirable. For example, a check written by George Washington for the purchase of a painting reveals his taste in art and his preference for a specific artist. All attributes of a check including date, payee, bank, and amount of a check may have interesting associations. Checks with intriguing connections or revealing information are often referred to as having significant content. Examples of authentic checks with meaningful associated content are included in this section.

Revolutionary leaders Fidel Castro and Che Guevara

Check written by Cuban leader Fidel Castro to comrade Ernesto "Che"Guevara shortly before the Cuban Missile Crisis. The association of these revolutionary icons inspires intrigue and imagination.

Franklin D. Roosevelt on D-Day

President Franklin D. Roosevelt signed this check bearing the date the Allied forces invaded Europe on June 6, 1944. As Commander-in-Chief of the United States Armed Forces, Roosevelt's association with D-Day has special historic significance.

D.H. Lawrence, Samuel Solomonovich Koteliansky, and *Lady Chatterley's Lover*

English author D.H. Lawrence receives a check from his friend and literary agent S.S. Koteliansky as payment for first edition copies of his famous book *Lady Chatterley's Lover*.

Thomas Jefferson and Monticello

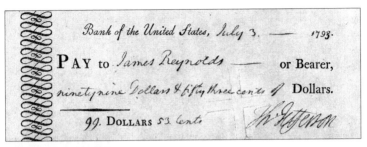

Thomas Jefferson wrote this check to Phila-delphia merchant James Reynolds for the purchase of large mirrors. Jefferson had the mirrors mounted in the parlor room of his home in Monticello. They were among the first large mirrors used in an American home, and they may have been inspired by Jefferson's visit to the Palace of Versailles in France.

John Lennon and Apple Records

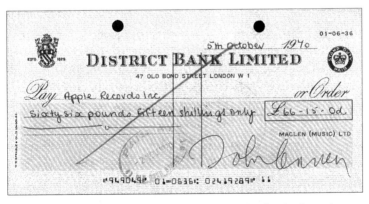

Check from John Lennon to Apple Records. In 1968, the Beatles formed Apple Records, and its first album was *Two Virgins* by John Lennon and Yoko Ono. *Yellow Submarine, Abbey Road,* and *Let it Be* are among many famous albums by the Beatles that were released by Apple. This check connects Apple Records, the Beatles, and John Lennon.

BILLS OF EXCHANGE

Bills of Exchange are a form of financial instrument designed to transfer money over long distances. Before modern electronic banking, private banks were reluctant to accept checks from other private banks without knowing if said checks were fraudulent or if sufficient funds were on deposit to cover the checks. Bills of Exchange were recognized by all bankers and used to transfer money to faraway places. Often, duplicate copies of Bills of Exchange were drafted (First, Second, Third, etc.) and sent by various means of transportation; if one Bill of Exchange was lost, another had a good chance of getting through.

FORGERIES

Some aficionados love to collect the interesting and unusual. Some philatelists, for instance, look for stamps with an inverted vignette, and some numismatists seek currency and/or coins that were imprinted or minted with errors. Among check collectors, there are those who seek fabricated documents that were skillfully created by famous philographic forgers. One of America's most notorious fakers was Joseph Cosey, infamously known for his brilliant forgeries of checks by Aaron Burr and Benjamin Franklin. Among the most collectible forged checks are those claimed to be from George Washington, but actually handwritten by the notorious Robert Spring.

NOTE:
Virtually anything signed with a ball-point pen and dated prior to 1935 or a felt-tip marker and dated prior to 1951 is a forgery.

Many of Spring's Washington bank checks are exposed in auction and proffered as forgeries. However, some of these forgeries are presented as genuine Washington-signed checks. Spring's forged signature of George Washington was often considerably smaller in size than that of the first president's actual signature.

George Washington Check Forgery

In the 1800s, master forger Robert Spring turned out thousands of counterfeit checks that skillfully mimicked Washington's stylized handwriting. All of Spring's holograph checks bearing Washington's forged signature, often represented as authentic, were drawn on the Office of Discount & Deposit, Baltimore.

Above, an authentic check from George Washington. From 1770 until the end of his life, Washington crossed the lower level of the "g" in his name and changed the "s" to a slanted line. He never signed checks with his full signature. During his adult life, Washington had accounts in at least three banks: Bank of Pennsylvania, Bank of Columbia, and the Bank of Alexandria.

Facsimile Signatures

It is important for collectors to be able to distinguish between checks that are genuinely signed and checks that are signed in facsimile by mechanical methods. Checks may have had a facsimile signature printed on it when it was produced, or placed on a check later by a device, such as a laser printer or hand stamp. Since the invention of rubber stamps by James Woodruff in 1864, stamps have been used to add logos, ornamental designs, and signatures to checks. Rubber-stamped signatures have appeared on checks since J.F.W. Dorman in Baltimore first commercialized them in 1865.

Keep in mind the following pearls to identify facsimile signatures on checks:

- Unlike genuine autographs, facsimile signatures do not soak through paper and produce a "show-through" effect. Also unlike genuine signatures, facsimile signatures are often created by a stamp and do not create an indent: a depression or chiseled recess in the surface of paper that occurs when the signer uses an ink pen with the normal degree of pressure
- Facsimile signatures usually have uniform coloration. Genuine signatures vary in coloration because of differing pressure points during the writing process.
- Facsimile signatures have a uniform edge where ink from the signature extends beyond the writing line and hesitating pressure points. Genuine ink signatures tend to bleed at their junctions.

Signature Facsimile Check

```
GRANTHAM INDUSTRIES INC.              El Segundo Office          Nº    4771
    600 LAIRPORT STREET        First Interstate Bank of California
    EL SEGUNDO, CA 90245            El Segundo, CA 90245              16-21/195
       213 - 772-7723                                                   1220

PAY    ********ONE THOUSAND AND NO/100********              DOLLARS
                                          DATE        NET CHECK
TO THE   M.I.T. ALUMNI ASSOCIATION      1-5-75        1,00000
ORDER OF


                                   Frederick W Grantham

⑈004771⑈ ⑆122000218⑈ 1959427081⑈        11
```

Frederick Grantham, inventor of the modern gas dryer, used a machine-printed signature on his business checks. The uniformity of his signature, without shading variations, is a telltale sign of a facsimile.

Facsimile Signature Methods
- Check imprint
- Machine printed
- Hand stamped
- Laser printed

CHAPTER 3

Finding & Purchasing Checks

THE HUNT

Antiques stores, flea markets, estate sales, used bookstores, autograph dealers, Internet auctions, and established auction houses are the main sources for check collectors. Dedicated collectors pursue all avenues, but you may decide to focus on just a few sources if you're building a collection slowly.

Antiques Shops

Sometimes antiques shops come in contact with estate liquidators who have access to documents that include old checks. It is a good idea to keep your name and interest on file with the best antiques dealers in your area.

Auctions

Auctions are primary sources for obtaining quality items for many check collectors. Purchasing checks at auction from your home or office through your computer or telephone is easy and convenient.

There can be a down side, however. At auction, there is always a possibility that a check will sell for much higher than normal market conditions. This happens when at least two bidders get caught up in a competitive battle over a particular item. If you buy a check at auction for a price far above normal levels, it becomes highly unlikely that you will ever be in similar circumstances again—or be able to re-sell the check at a high price. The lesson bidders need to remember is that in the heated frenzy of an auction, emotions may influence your buying judgment.

Check collectors have a certain security when they purchase from an auction company operating with a state license. The state regulatory agency for auctioneers may be called on to settle a dispute between a bidder and the auctioneer. However, a state agency may defer a request to settle a dispute if the item in question was purchased more than a year ago. In addition, some state licensing boards, such as New Hampshire's, require that the bidder be available for on-site hearings in their state of jurisdiction.

KNOW YOUR LIMITS!
Billionaire Malcolm Forbes loved to collect autographs from notable personalities. One of his favorite auction houses was R.M. Smythe in New York City. Although he could well afford almost anything, he told the auctioneer to "let it go" when he believed the bidding prices became excessive.

Collecting Societies

Meetings and leads for trade shows that offer a variety of checks are often published in newsletters of various check collecting organizations. See the Resources chapter for more information on these groups.

Dealers

Checks with revenue stamps or imprints may sometimes be found in the inventory of stamp dealers. You can find these dealers in your local yellow pages, as well as in trade magazines and at trade shows.

Estate Sales

Regularly check Craigslist and/or your local newspaper for information on estate sales. It is not uncommon to discover shoeboxes full of old checks.

Many experts say that the first known appearance of the dollar sign was in 1797, but the date of this check—1796—contradicts that claim. This may be one of the earliest, if not the oldest, existing checks with a dollar sign.

Flea Markets

Dealers of all types bring their wares to the flea market. Ask to see their "paper." Sometimes a seller at a flea market will pull out a shoebox full of antique checks, and these just might prove to be a treasure trove. Flea markets are held in many cities across the United States. Check Google, your local newspaper, *Paper Pile Quarterly*, and/or *Antique & Collectables Monthly Newsmagazine* for schedules of flea markets in your area. Don't be discouraged if you don't find old checks during the first few visits to a flea market. With persistence, your efforts may well be handsomely rewarded.

Online

The Internet has greatly expanded commerce for collectibles. Collectors are discovering that checks of all types and from all over the world may be sought and purchased through the Internet. Check collectors usually seek cancelled checks, but many memorabilia collectors also pursue unused specimen checks and/or blank checks for their historic value as contemporary examples of financial printing. Some memorabilia collectors also find old checkbooks and bank statements to be desirable mementos.

Trade Shows

Coin, paper money, and antiques shows are often useful venues for seeking old checks. You can search online for upcoming shows and put yourself on mailing lists to keep abreast of events.

THE LEGAL ISSUES

Get It in Writing

The Statute of Frauds (Uniform Commercial Code Section 2-201) dictates that any fraud charges stemming from the sale of goods for an amount over $500 are not enforceable unless the transaction has a written record that is signed by the buyer and seller. Because of this, make sure that any transaction you make for amounts above $500 is recorded in writing. While the finalized contract need not have an original signature, the parties must be identified and documentation that both parties accepted the terms of the transaction is required. The final requirement of this code is that the contract must specify the quantity in the transaction. Therefore, whether you buy one or a thousand checks, please make sure to report the quantity in the written receipt.

Sellers are entitled to their opinion regarding the desirability or value of a check. This may be construed as a statement of opinion rather than an expressed warranty. Again, a clear written contract is the best way to avoid confusion and conflict.

Authenticity

The Uniform Commercial Code section 2-725 gives the buyer four years from the date of sale to legally contest an item that has been guaranteed authentic by the seller. However, authentication of autographs is a murky area; so-called experts can and do disagree on the validity of autographs. Contesting the authenticity of a celebrity signature may quickly become a no-win situation, so don't bring such charges lightly.

Price & Value

Oscar Wilde once said, "A cynic is a man who knows the price of everything and the value of nothing." It is important that all check collectors can distinguish price from value.

The price of an item, whether it's one written on a dealer list, stated verbally by a flea-market dealer, or achieved through bidding at an auction, should not be confused with that item's value. Prices for similar checks may vary considerably from one dealer to another and from one auction to another. The price of a check is dependent on the seller's audience at that moment and may be greatly influenced by trends or fads. Often, the seller describes a check as "scarce" or "rare" to justify a high price. It is important for check collectors to understand that scarcity in isolation neither creates demand nor increases value.

Legally speaking, fair-market value is what a willing purchaser will pay a willing seller in an open market. The basis for this definition is cited in the California case Kaiser Co. v. Reid (1947), 30 C2d, 184 P2d 879. "Fair" in legal terms means "honest" rather than "average" or "median." This definition of *fair* was cited in the California case East Bay Municipal Utility District v. Kieffler (1929), 99 CA 240, 278 P 476, 279 P 178.

The paragraph above provides the legal definition of "value." But practically speaking, for a collector of any kind, "value" means that you are seeking a durable investment that has the potential for appreciation. A check collector who seeks value will purchase quality checks at a reasonable price that have the potential for long-term appreciation. When you are deciding what price to pay for a check, consider its long-term value, which really means its long-term chance of appreciation.

Of course, "value" also means an item's value to you personally. Every collector has at least a few pieces that bear a high personal value, even if the likelihood of significant appreciation isn't great. The point is to be aware of what is important to you as a collector.

ENJOY THE RESEARCH

It's important to remember why collecting checks can be so enjoyable. It's not just about the dollar value and the rarity. Much of the reward comes from the research involved in learning about a check and its provenance. Don't sell this process short—take your time and enjoy it. Learn about the relationship between the check writer and the recipient. What were some of the significant historic events going on at that time that might have impacted the parties involved? Or perhaps the events weren't significant, but they could still be fascinating. What did the check say about the concerns and priorities of the check writer? What was going on at the bank during that time?

Spending time researching a check that interests you provides a focused window into the past that can reveal all sorts of engaging stories and connections.

CHAPTER 4

Storing & Maintaining Checks

"It is the duty of every good citizen to use all the opportunities, which occur to him, for preserving documents relating to the history of our country."
— Thomas Jefferson

Jefferson's point is essential for all collectors: You must keep your collection safe from injury, harm, or destruction. Doing so will ensure many years of enjoyment and collecting pleasure for you and future generations of collectors, not to mention help preserve historical records.

THE BASICS OF PAPER

Paper is a sheet of interwoven fibers made of rag, wood, or grass. Parchment and vellum are made of animal skin. Plant-based papers contain lignin, which gives a plant strength—but which leads to the degradation and yellowing of the paper over time. Therefore, quality papers have the lignin removed. (Cheap newsprint has lignin, which is why newspapers yellow so dramatically with age.) Light and heat also cause the acceleration of the aging processes in paper, causing it to become more acidic. Increased acidity results in paper degradation and brittleness. Also dangerous is humidity, which promotes mold and mildew growth in paper, and may also cause rusting of the minute amounts of iron found in paper. This rusting process is known as "foxing."

Ink is a colored substance for writing and printing. Lampblack, also known as carbon black, is fine powdered black soot resulting from the incomplete combustion of materials containing carbon; it is commonly used in toner for laser printers and photocopiers. Excess exposure to light causes both ink and carbon black to fade.

Checks written before 1850 were usually written on paper with "chain lines"—a pattern of lines embedded in the paper caused by pressing the paper pulp during processing. Cheap wood-pulp paper was rarely used for checks and, if so, not until about 1845.

PRINCIPLES OF PRESERVATION

An important consideration for the accumulation of any significant collection is the care of your paper documents to maintain their vibrancy and longevity. Harm to your collection may arise from exposure to acid, heat, light, moisture, and mistreatment. Many experts consider prolonged exposure to acid as the most damaging menace to paper collectibles.

Here are a few essential rules:

- Handle checks with clean hands.
- Maintain your checks in Mylar-D sleeve containers.
- Store your collection in an environment with little or no light.
- Maintain your collection in an environment with little humidity and a moderate temperature.
- Never use ordinary Scotch tape or glue to repair a defect on checks. Over time Scotch tape or ordinary glue will discolor and destroy paper.

ENEMIES OF PRESERVATION

Careless handling
Contact with acidic materials
Ultraviolet light
High temperatures
Adverse humidity
Molds & fungi
Air pollution

Several sprays are commercially available for de-acidifying paper checks. However, many conservationists caution against routine de-acidification of paper collectibles. It may cause uneven aging of the paper, resulting in blotches or discoloration. Consulting with a qualified conservator may help determine if de-acidification of your check is a good idea.

CATALOGING

Collectors who accumulate a substantial number of checks will need to maintain a systematic and readily accessible inventory. A simple index card system works just fine, but collectors who have some computer literacy may be better off having a computerized database.

A properly designed database allows for easy searching and sorting, and it serves as a storage record that can be easily duplicated for backup. Many commercially available computer database programs will meet the needs of the check collector.

At the very least, your database should have this information:

· Last name
· First name
· Price paid
· Date of acquisition
· Type of document (i.e. check, draft, promissory note)
· Revenue stamp classification
· Condition
· Place of purchase
· Detailed description
· Commentary

ARCHIVAL MAINTENANCE

Robert Spence, a former president of the *American Society of Check Collectors* wrote, "Preservation of checks is the most important part of check collecting." By preserving checks we preserve a moment of history that may be passed on from one generation of collector to the next. The devoted collector has a responsibility for maintaining his collection in the best possible condition for others to share and enjoy. Indeed, many of the checks available to collectors today are here only because of the thoughtful collecting habits of check collectors in the past.

Plastic Holders

Holders for preserving and displaying checks should be clear and acid-free, permit easy and repeated handling, and should not emit by-products that damage paper.

The best all-purpose protective containers for paper documents are Mylar-D check holders manufactured by Dupont Corporation. Unlike many other types of plastics, Mylar-D is an inert archival material that will not damage paper. Mylar-D check holders are also thick enough to withstand repeated handling.

Mylar-D check holders are available in different sizes. Although they are crystal clear, you can sometimes see a reflection of a bluish ripple resembling oil on water when they are exposed to light. The size that accommodates most checks and allows for easy insertion and removal is about 9 5/8 by 4 ¼ inches. For very large, oversize checks, a Mylar-D page protector placed in a three-ring archival binder or acid-free archival box will provide suitable protection.

Glassine envelopes, commonly used to store stamps, and black photographic mounting paper, which is readily available at most retail outlets, are highly acidic and will damage checks. Polyvinylchloride (PVC) plastic holders are another material to avoid. This type of plastic degrades when exposed to light and heat, resulting in by-products that cause the deterioration of paper.

The use of lamination for storage is controversial. Lamination is not generally recommended, because toxic by-products from paper may accumulate after being sealed by lamination, and this can hurt the paper. In addition, the process of lamination may damage paper.

Paper items can sometimes be very difficult to remove from a laminated holder.

An acid-free archival box for check storage provides a convenient and inexpensive method for filing checks. The Resources chapter in this book has a list of vendors who supply Mylar-D check holders and archival storage boxes.

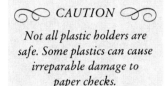

CAUTION

Not all plastic holders are safe. Some plastics can cause irreparable damage to paper checks.

DISPLAYING YOUR COLLECTION

Checks can be very attractive when displayed in frames, especially when coordinated photographs associated with some aspect of the check are included in the display—say, perhaps, a check signed by Abraham Lincoln with a photograph of the former president. Care must be taken, however, to display these valuable items without harm.

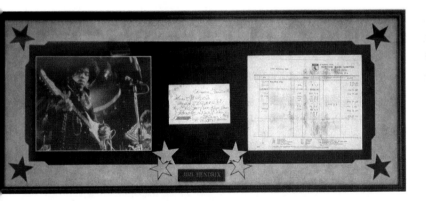

Checks framed in an artful and archival setting can make an attractive display with conversational interest. This check from guitarist Jimi Hendrix is framed with his photograph and his bank statement showing a corresponding entry for the check. Hendrix used this check to pay for recordings by George Handel. The next day, Hendrix went to Olympic Studios to record Bob Dylan's classic song *All Along the Watchtower*.

Your check should not be folded, cut, or altered in any way to fit into a mat or frame. The frame may be either wood or metal. However, a wood frame should have a lining to prevent chemicals in the wood from transferring to the contents of the display.

Lignans are fibers that are common in the plant kingdom. They can break down into fatty acids and hormone-like chemical compounds called phytoestrogens, thereby damaging paper.

The supporting board and covering mat should be made of acid-free inert material. Most conservationists recommend the use of 100% ragboard as the safest material for backboard and matting. Color in the mat board should not bleed or rub off. Ordinary cardboard should not be used in frame displays, since it emits peroxides and toxic chemicals derived from the breakdown of lignin. These materials stain paper with a characteristic yellow discoloration.

Hinges and other devices used to fixate the position of checks in a display should also be composed of acid-free material. Checks may be safely secured to a mat with Japanese rice paper and wheat or starch paste. Cellophane (Scotch) tape, masking tape, linen tape, surgical tape, and regular plastic tape should all be avoided, because they can damage paper.

A glazed front of a framed display should consist of either UV glass or UV acrylic sheet (e.g., Plexiglas ®, Lucite ®, Perspex ®, Lexan ®) to screen out glare and harmful ultraviolet light. Be sure that the glazing does not come into contact with the check.

Moisture that condenses on the backside of glazing may be transferred to a check and cause water stains. Furthermore, photos on checks may adhere to the glazing. To prevent these problems, checks should be recessed from the glazed material in a matted well. Keep in mind that UV-filtered glazing will reduce but not completely eliminate damage caused by visible light.

Avoid hanging your framed check on the interior face of a wall that is exposed to the outdoors. Moisture may be transferred through the wall and affect your check. Also avoid hanging framed checks near stoves, fireplaces, radiators, in direct sunlight, and in places with extremes in temperature and humidity.

The information given in this section is of a general nature and has been recommended by the Library of Congress in the care of its collections. Collectors should consult with a qualified conservator for their specific requirements.

CHAPTER 5

What's It Worth?

Beauty is in the eye of the beholder, and perhaps the same may be said of the valuation of checks. What appeals to one check collector may not interest another. To a great extent, value is subject to interpretation. Still, it can be defined: Value in check collecting relates to the intrinsic worth of an item and the potential for long-term appeal.

CHECK CHARACTERISTICS

The value of a check depends on a number of characteristics. The most important of these factors include:

- Stature of the check writer
- Condition
- Rarity
- Date
- Signature quality
- Content
- Supply & demand

Stature of the Check Writer

Checks that have been signed by personalities who have made significant contributions tend to retain the best value over time. Checks signed by such important notables as Susan B. Anthony, George Washington, Neil Armstrong, Francis Crick, or Ralph Waldo Emerson will probably always be in demand. These are examples of signatures that have "permanent value."

Although checks signed by movie and television stars may be desirable in the short term, they do not always retain long-term appeal. Shining stars from the silent era of silver screen may have been the rave during their time, but many have since drifted into obscurity. For example, checks signed by entertainer Joe Jefferson, the most popular comic actor in America during the 19th century, were at one time worth more than those signed by Thomas Jefferson; today, they have considerably less appeal. That said, there is a small group of dedicated check collectors with a special interest in television and movie stars, as well as collectors intent on collecting every available check, and these people seek checks signed by entertainment personalities.

Exceptions are limited to stars associated with true classic movies. Actors and actresses in classic movies have lasting appeal and are always in demand. For example, personalities associated with *Gone with the Wind* or *The Wizard of Oz* are perpetual favorites because these movies appeal to successive generations of audiences.

One of the best ways to judge lasting appeal is to review the content of elementary and high school textbooks. Textbooks influence generation after generation of check collectors: History textbooks describe important figures involved in the American Revolution and the Civil War, science textbooks describe researchers who made groundbreaking experiments, and classic novels are written by authors who will be remembered for many years to come.

The important individuals we are exposed to as young students make an indelible impression that remain with us for the rest of our lives. Our early impressions become the nostalgia that motivates collectors in adulthood—at a time when we may be able to afford to collect mementos and treasured relics of the past. The important individuals illustrated in our textbooks represent the "blue chips" for autograph check collectors.

Condition

The importance of a check's condition brings to mind the advice given for purchasing quality real estate: "location, location, location." For checks, the mantra is "condition, condition, condition." For the serious check collector, hardly any other factor is as important.

Checks that have been damaged by mildew, bug or rodent bites, excessive folds or tears, or water lose their aesthetic appeal. Damaged checks are nearly worthless to collectors, unless the check has historic significance or is signed by an important individual.

The collector should seek checks that are in the best possible condition. Whenever possible, select checks that do not have cancellation marks that affect the signature, vignette, or other interesting areas. Checks with extraneous handwriting, including mathematical calculations, detract from the appearance and should be avoided.

Checks signed by famous people who are notable enough to be described in textbooks are likely to appeal to successive generations of collectors.

Tears in checks may either be open or closed. Open tears, which involve loss of paper, negatively affect the appearance of a check. Closed tears are cuts without loss of paper. The worst type of closed tear is that which separates portions of a check; for instance, a check that has been folded and opened repeatedly will often develop a tear that bisects the check. Both types of tears often require expert restoration.

Unless there are mitigating circumstances, collectors should avoid checks that have excessive cancellations, staple holes, and perforations, especially when these markings affect important areas of the check.

Grading

Condition is essential when determining the value of a check. The following grading system helps clarify the communication between buyers and sellers:

- Mint – No blemishes or defects. May often be found in unused checks.
- Fine – Up to a few minor blemishes, such as a bent corner or superficial abrasion, but these blemishes do not affect important areas of the check.

· Very Good – Up to a few moderate defects, such as a fold, excess markings, or cancellations; these may affect important areas of a check.
· Good – Up to a few significant defects that affect important areas of a check.
· Fair –Significant defects, paper loss, or obliteration of any portion of a check.

Rarity

Checks with revenue stamps, checks written for unusually high or low amounts, rarely seen celebrity-signed checks, and checks from important banks or companies no longer in existence tend to be more in demand and therefore more valuable.

It is important for the check collector to not confuse rarity with desirability. Certain checks are incredibly rare but are not necessarily worth a lot of money. For example, checks from Albany, New York dated 1909 may be rare, but they will probably never rise to the top of the collecting charts. On the other hand, checks signed by Isaac Newton rarely come to market. Rarity of availability, with the added historic significance and signature of a notable person, means that a check signed by Isaac Newton would represent a most infrequent opportunity for a collector to acquire a masterpiece.

Date

Dates are only important when they are associated with the check writer or the events of the day. For example, a handwritten check from Abraham Lincoln during the height of the Civil War may have greater appeal than a check he wrote just prior to the conflict. A check written by Marilyn Monroe on her birthday may have greater appeal than a check written on any other day. The significance of the date on a check is in direct proportion to its association with the check writer and corresponding events.

Content

A check is referred to as having significant content when there is an interesting or meaningful relationship among various features of a check. Relationships between payor, payee, bank, and the date of a check, are important features that determine the content value of a check.

Supply & Demand

The price of checks is similar to many other collectibles. Checks may be purchased for anywhere between five cents to $25,000. Supply and demand are the key factors that determine the price you pay. As you may remember from your Introduction to Economics class, the principle of supply and demand is a simple one: Sellers determine supply and buyers determine demand. The quantity of sellers, buyers, and checks are the variables that determine the availability and prices of checks, and the number of buyers willing and able to purchase checks determines the demand. The relationship between demand and supply is inversely proportionate; if the supply does not keep up with demand, the price of a check rises. Prices drop when the supply of a specific check outweighs demand.

Checks signed by modern entertainment celebrities have been in plentiful supply. As a result, the prices of these checks have remained relatively constant for the past decade despite consistent demand. On the other hand, checks signed by historic figures, including Thomas Jefferson, Abraham Lincoln, and Albert Einstein, have continued to escalate in value because of constant demand from affluent check collectors able to afford increasing prices for a very limited supply of these desirable autographed checks.

Content often transforms an ordinary check into a gem of history. Part of the fun of collecting is the research that uncovers unexpected names and relationships.

Signature Quality

Signatures of famous people are often worth considerably more than the checks they grace. However, a blemished signature may significantly reduce the value of the check. Cancellation marks that mar the signature detract from the value. Punch-hole cancellations, if extensive, may almost completely obscure the signature. Rubber-stamp impressions are also notorious for defacing important writing on checks.

The purist check collector with an interest in autographs will avoid checks where the signature is affected with cancellation marks, especially when unblemished examples are available. When purchasing a check for its autograph, look for minimal cancellations and legible handwriting.

Pen quills or fountain pens were used to sign checks prior to the 1940s. The most commonly used fountain pens were those manufactured by Waterman, Parker, Sheaffer, and Wahl-Eversharp. Inks for these pens were usually black or dark blue when first applied, but they turn brown over time.

Many of the autographs written by quill or fountain pen have a halo or feathering caused by the migration of the liquid vehicle (usually linseed oil) that carried the ink pigment (usually lamp black, also known as carbon black).

John J. Loud of Weymouth, Massachusetts in 1888, held the earliest patent for a ballpoint pen. Paul Eisner and Frank Klimes in Prague, Czechoslovakia invented the modern ballpoint pen around 1935. The first commercially successful ballpoint pen was manufactured in 1945, and signatures made with ballpoints started appearing in the 1950s.

Signatures created with carbon black and oil tend to withstand fading. Inks that have bright colors based on synthetic dyes can fade over time. Therefore, if given a choice, black ink signatures on checks are usually preferable to blue or other ink colors.

CHECKS AS INVESTMENTS

The vast majority of check collecting aficionados purchase checks because of the joy of collecting. Each one brings a wonderful opportunity for education and enjoyment. The amount of work involved in finding, maintaining, and holding checks for an opportune selling time makes check collecting dubious as an investment vehicle for most amateurs. Only dealers with well-established supply lines and outlets for ready sale are equipped to sell checks for a steady profit.

To be a true investment, a check must appreciate in value. Checks signed by notable blue-chip personalities will probably never go out of style. Similarly, checks with historic significance, interesting attributes, or nostalgic or sentimental value—as well as those bearing revenue stamps or drawn on the accounts of famous companies—will continue to be sought by check collectors.

How the value of your check collection will fare over time is difficult to forecast. It will be influenced by supply and demand, market activity, general economic conditions, rarity, and fashion. As former Yankee baseball player Yogi Berra says, "It's tough to make predictions, especially about the future."

SELLING YOUR CHECKS

Selling checks may be just as exciting as buying checks. Finding a good home for duplicates, a change in your interests, and liquidation to meet expenses are all good reasons for selling or trading parts or all of your collection.

Many collectors sell their checks directly to other collectors. A written description, statement of condition, and, when possible, a photograph should provide a full disclosure of the check. A check that is carefully described will help prevent buyer dissatisfaction. Checks should be shipped only upon receipt and clearance of payment, unless the seller is absolutely certain of the buyer's credit reliability.

Collectors may also sell to dealers who specialize in checks, revenue stamps, and/or autographs. The prospect of a quick and hassle-free transaction with an established dealer is the primary reason why collectors sell directly to dealers. Any transaction of significance should include a simple contract to document the items and terms of the sale.

Consignment to an auction house or dealer means that you are transferring the legal right to another party to sell your item. Be sure that you agree to the terms and conditions of the consignment before sending your items. The terms should clearly specify if your consignment is exclusive or may be offered through additional sources. Auction houses usually require that the consignor give them exclusive rights to sell consigned items.

The length of the consignment, the commission rate, and the terms for transferring title are important considerations. Auction houses usually charge a commission of 10% to 25% of the sales price. Auction houses may also charge you for illustrations of your check for their catalog and shipping and for items that do not sell.

Your personal checks, especially those drawn on well-known banks that no longer exist, may well become collectible checks of the future.

It's important that you clearly understand all auction charges and the deadline for your payment, and make sure the auction house has fire and theft insurance before consignment. All of the terms between you and the auction house need to be specified in a written contract, and some points are negotiable.

Be sure that title to your check does not pass to either the dealer or a buyer until you have been paid in full. If the auction house sells and releases your item to a non-paying buyer, you may not recover the item or your payment unless your prior agreement protects you. You have a legal right to sue the buyer, but the auction house is under no legal obligation to enforce collection.

It is also important to note that auction houses usually have ultimate discretion regarding how your check is described to the public and how it is visually presented and catalogued.

If you are concerned that your consignment may not sell for the minimum price you are willing to accept, be sure that you and the dealer or auction house agree on a reserve price. The reserve is a confidential rock-bottom price for your check.

Other avenues available for selling checks include direct sale to autograph or philatelic dealers, advertising in trade magazines, and offering your checks at flea markets. You may either set up your own booth at a flea market or make arrangements with a trustworthy flea market dealer to sell your checks for a modest commission. Flea-market sales have their own peculiarities, so you should familiarize yourself with those before jumping into this adventure.

Tax implications

Check collectors who buy items for personal enjoyment must pay local and state sales taxes on their acquisitions. Collectors must also pay tax on income they earn from their collections but are not permitted to claim losses they may incur. However, collectors who show an earnest attempt to buy and sell checks with the goal of profit may qualify as dealers.

Check dealers pay tax at ordinary income tax rates and may deduct losses to offset gains. As a check dealer, you must record every sale and issue an invoice to every buyer. Consult your tax advisor for further information on this subject.

> ❧ *DISCLAIMER:* ❧
> *All the prices have been compiled from the most reliable sources, and every effort has been made to eliminate errors and questionable data. The author, publisher, or bookseller will not be held responsible for losses that may occur in the purchase, sale, or other transaction of items because of information contained in this book. Readers who feel they have discovered errors are invited to write and inform us, so we may correct them in subsequent editions.*

PRICE GUIDE

The prices shown in the following tables are general prices for celebrity-signed checks. The prices assume that the check is in very good to excellent condition. They also assume that the celebrity has signed on the front (recto). Endorsed checks that are signed on the back (verso) are not nearly as desirable and are often shunned by many collectors. Condition and content may greatly influence value. For example, a check signed by Fidel Castro to Che Guevara for services in the Cuban government, especially if endorsed by Guevara, would have considerably greater value than a simple check signed by Fidel Castro to a temporary employee.

> *REMEMBER:*
> *The market valuation is only meaningful to the extent that there is a willing buyer at a given price.*

Of course, there are many more readily available celebrity checks than are included in this list. And remember that supply and demand greatly influence prices of checks. If a hoard is discovered, for instance, prices can drop by a considerable margin. Prices vary with every market, and external events often influence current market value. For example, a popular television documentary on the Civil War may temporarily elevate the interest in (and prices of) Civil War–related checks.

Commonly Available Signed Checks

Bud Abbott	$750
John Q. Adams	$1,250
Buzz Aldrin	$250
Muhammad Ali	$1,100
Benjamin Altman	$175
Desi Arnaz	$150
Chester Arthur	$1,250
Turner Ashby	$2,500
Stephen Austin	$3,500
Lucille Ball	$250
Mildred Benson	$125
Moe Berg	$450
Irving Berlin	$750
Lenny Bruce	$1,250
Raymond Burr	$75
Edgar Rice Burroughs	$150
Francis X. Bushman	$75
Richard E. Byrd	$175
Truman Capote	$750
Jimmy Carter	$150
Joshua Chamberlain	$1,750
Roberto Clemente	$2,750
Charles Conrad	$150
Ty Cobb	$1,250
Calvin Coolidge	$450
James F. Cooper	$150
Lou Costello	$125
Marion Davies	$150
Cecil B. DeMille	$125
Joe DiMaggio	$550
Walt Disney	$1,850

Tommy Dorsey	$175
Thomas Edison	$1,500
Albert Einstein	$6,500
W.C. Fields	$410
Bobby Fisher	$385
Errol Flynn	$375
Clark Gable	$450
Alexander Gardner	$3,450
Judy Garland	$525
Charles Goodyear	$750
John Gotti	$1,200
Gus Grissom	$1,250
Jack Haley	$75
Florence Harding	$225
Warren G. Harding	$1,650
George Hartford	$200
Gabby Hartnett	$195
Ben Hogan	$165
Moe Howard	$235
James Irwin	$150
Kate Jackson	$45
Thomas Jefferson	$9,500
Walter Johnson	$1,250
John Kennedy	$6,500
Jack Kerouac	$1,250
Walter Lantz	$75
Stan Laurel	$225
John Lennon	$5,500
Charles Lindbergh	$1,750
Vincent Lombardi	$150
Jack London	$350
Jack Lord	$50
Sal Maglie	$35
Billy Martin	$450

The least expensive presidential check is one from Jimmy Carter; the most valuable is from Zachary Taylor.

Groucho Marx	$250
Zeppo Marx	$125
Tom Mix	$250
Marilyn Monroe	$2,250
Richard Nixon	$4,250
Maxfield Parrish	$290
Tim Pickering	$420
Vincent Price	$75
Ronald Reagan	$850
Al Ringling	$330
Henry Ringling	$385
Edward G. Robinson	$85
George Romero	$55
Linda Ronstadt	$55
Theodore Roosevelt	$1,750
Jack Ruby	$250
Rosalind Russell	$40
Babe Ruth	$3,250
Wally Schirra	$65
Rod Serling	$250
Ernest Shackleton	$1,750
Daniel Sickles	$115
Duke Snider	$75
Edward Stanton	$350
Charles Steinmetz	$125
Frederick von Steuben	$1,500
Robert L. Stevenson	$1,750
Leopold Stokowski	$75
Sharon Stone	$85
Barbra Streisand	$125

Erich von Stroheim	$115
John Sutter	$8,500
Alfred L. Tennyson	$350
Smith Thompson	$115
Harry Truman	$650
Rudy Vallee	$45
Alberta Varga	$350
Fred Vinson	$65
George Washington	$28,000
Mae West	$145
Brian Wilson	$125
Orville Wright	$1,250
Thomas Wolfe	$1,250
Hoyt Wilhelm	$140
Alvin York	$450

Exceptionally Rare Celebrity-Signed Checks

The celebrity-signed checks shown below are rarely seen on the autograph market. For example, only one check each signed by George Custer, Jimi Hendrix, and Zachary Taylor has been offered for auction in the past twenty years.

John Adams	$12,500
Alexander G. Bell	$3,500
John Wilkes Booth	$23,500
Fidel Castro	$15,500
David Crockett	$17,500
George Custer	$23,000
Dwight Eisenhower	$7,500
Ben Franklin	$19,500
Lou Gehrig	$15,500
Alexander Hamilton	$8,500
Oliver Hardy	$1,250
Jimi Hendrix	$18,500
Harry Houdini	$6,500
Jacqueline Kennedy	$4,500
John Locke	$28,500
Ted Maiman	$3,500
Isaac Newton	$32,000
Edgar Allen Poe	$28,500
John Slaughter	$1,750
Jeb Stuart	$24,500
Zachary Taylor	$32,500

Rarely obtainable American presidential checks include those written by John Adams, Zachary Taylor, John Tyler, Dwight Eisenhower, and Lyndon Johnson.

CHAPTER 6

Resources

INSURANCE

Collectibles Insurance Agency
P.O. Box 1200-PM
Westminster, Maryland 21158
(888) 837-9537, fax (410) 876-9233
www.collectinsure.com

Offers insurance on collections. See the online application and rate quotes on the website.

ORGANIZATIONS

American Society of Check Collectors
473 East Elm
Sycamore, IL 60178-1934
www.ascheckcollectors.org

A nonprofit organization dedicated to check collecting. This society publishes *The Check Collector* on a quarterly basis.

British Banking History Society
38 Ingleton Road
Newsome, Huddersfield
West Yorkshire HD4 6QX
United Kingdom
www.banking-history.co.uk

Founded in 1980, this organization focuses on the history of check collecting and banking. It publishes *Counterfoil* on a quarterly basis, and its website has an informative collection of articles.

Society of Paper Money Collectors, Inc.

P.O. Box 2331
Chapel Hill, NC 27515-2331
www.spmc.org

Founded in 1961 and incorporated in 1964 in the District of Columbia as a nonprofit organization, the Society of Paper Money Collectors has more than 1,750 members from around the world. Membership is open to anyone interested in paper money or related areas, including checks, stocks, engravings, and other fiscal ephemera. For information on joining, contact Frank Clark, membership director, P.O. Box 117060, Carrollton, TX 75011.

Universal Autograph Collectors Club

P.O. Box 1392
Mount Dora, FL 32756
www.uacc.org

A nonprofit organization founded in 1965, this club is dedicated to the hobby of collecting autographs. It is one of the largest autograph organizations in the world.

PUBLICATIONS

The American Revenuer
Kenneth Trettin
P.O. Box 56
Rockford, IA 50468-0056
(641) 756-3542, e-mail: hogman@omnitelcom.com

This philatelic journal, published six times a year, publishes occasional articles regarding bank checks and revenue stamps.

Antique & Collectables Monthly Newsmagazine
500 Fesler, Suite 201; P.O. Box 12589
El Cajon, CA 92022
Editorial: (619) 593-2933 , show information: (619) 593-2927
e-mail: ac@krause.com

This is a great resource for finding schedules and locations of trade shows and flea markets around the country. National distribution.

The Check Collector
The Journal of The American Society of Check Collectors
473 East Elm
Sycamore, IL 60178-1934
www.ascheckcollectors.org

Paper Pile Quarterly
P.O. Box 337
San Anselmo, CA 94979
(415) 454-5552, e-mail: apaperpile@aol.com

A great resource for finding schedules for flea market sales.

West Coast Peddler
P.O. Box 5134
Whittier, CA 90607
(562) 698-1718
www.westcoastpeddler.com; e-mail: westcoastpeddler@earthlink.net

This monthly publicaiton lists auctions and flea market sales.

SUPPLIES

This is a list of suppliers of archival material useful for the maintenance of your check collection. Fortunately, check collecting requires a minimum of supplies. The most useful supplies include enclosures for checks, plastic sleeves and acid-free boxes. Inclusion of the following companies does not constitute an endorsement of their products.

Bill M. Cole Enterprises
P.O. Box 60, Dept. JE
Randolph, MA 02368-0060
(800) 225-8249, (781) 986-2656
www.bcemylar.com

Supplier of a variety of archival products including archival frame displays.

Cohasco, Inc.
Document Preservation Center
Postal 821
Yonkers, New York 10702
(914) 476-8500, fax (914) 476-8573
http://cohascodpc.com

Archival storage supplies

Conservation Resources International
8000-H Forbes Place
Springfield, VA 22151
(800) 624-6932, fax (703) 321-0629
www.conservationresources.com

Denly's of Boston
P.O. Box 51010
Boston, MA 02205
(617) 482-8477
www.denlys.com

Supplier of Mylar-D check holders.

Light Impressions Inc.
10425 Slusher Drive
Santa Fe Springs, CA 90670
(800) 828-6216, e-mail: info@lightimpressionsdirect.com
www.lightimpresionsdirect.com

Supplies top-loading polyester check holders, mat boards, display albums, and picture frames.

Oregon Paper Money Exchange
6802 SW 33rd Place
Portland, OR 97219
(503) 245-3659
www.opme.web.aplus.net

Supplier of Mylar-D check holders.

Subway Stamp Shop Inc.
2121 Beale Avenue
Altoona, PA 16601
(800) 221-9960, (814) 946-1000
e-mail: custserv@subwaystamp.com
www.subwaystamp.com

Established in 1931, this company supplies opaque glassine and clear ProLar archival top-loading check holders.

University Products
517 Main Street, P.O. Box 101
Holyoke, MA 01041
(413) 532-9431
www.universityproducts.com
Supplier of a wide variety of archival products.

RESTORATION & CONSERVATION

Paper documents, especially if valuable, may require professional assistance to restore and maintain their viability.

"Restoration" refers to a process whereby the item is returned to a former state. "Conservation" refers to methods to keep an item from decaying. "Refurbish" means renovating an item, often with the goal of making it as if new.

Andrea Pitsch
348 West 36th Street
New York, NY 10018
(212) 594-9676, e-mail: apnyc@interport.net

Expert paper conservation.

Iowa Conservation and Preservation Consortium

Nancy Kraft
University of Iowa Libraries
Iowa City, IA 52242-1420
web/grinnell/edu/individuals/stuhrr/icpa/archivco.html

Offers a list of professional conservators.

Lower Hudson Conference of Historical Agencies & Museums

Tenna Harnik, Director
2199 Saw Mill River Road
Elmsford, NY 10523
(914) 592-6726
www.lowerhudsonconference.org

A nonprofit organization serving the Northeast United States since 1979, the Lower Hudson Conference maintains a list of professional conservators for restoring paper documents.

Northeast Document Conservation

Mary Todd Glaser, Director of Paper Conservation
100 Brickstone Square
Andover, MA 01810-1420
(978) 470-1010

WEBSITES

www.famous-celebrity-autographs.com

This website has the largest collection of celebrity signed check images on the Internet. Images of historic checks, checks from prominent companies, checks signed by famous people, and numerous informative articles about check collecting, are provided for education or purchase. This website also buys original checks signed by notable and famous personalities.

www.banktech.com

A commercial website that has useful information about upcoming check and electronic payment technology.

www.rdhinstl.com

An informative, non-commercial website produced by Bob Hohertz, president of the American Society of Check Collectors. This beautifully illustrated site explains the development and classification of American two-cent revenue stamps.

References

1. Armstrong, Leroy, and Denny, J.O. *Financial California. An Historical Review of the Beginnings and Progress of Banking in the State*. New York: Arno Press, 1980

2. Baynes-Cope, A.D. *Caring for Books and Documents*. New York: New Amsterdam Books. Published in Association with The British Library, 1981. This is a practical guide to maintaining paper documents authored by a former Scientific Officer in the British Museum Research Laboratory.

3. Castenholz, Bill J. *An Introduction to Revenue Stamps*. Pacific Palisades: Castenholz & Sons, 1994. Illustrated history of American revenue stamps.

4. Booker, John. *Travellers' Money*. New Hampshire: Alan Sutton Publishing, 1994. Scholarly study of the development of monetary arrangements used by travelers.

5. Dodd, Agnes F. *History of Money in the British Empire & the United States*. New York, Bombay, and Calcutta: Longmans, Green and Co., 1911.

6. Donovan, Gail. *The Story of Checks and Electronic Payments*. New York: Federal Reserve Bank of New York, 1995.

7. Fisher, A.W., McKenney, J.L. *The Development of the ERMA banking system: lessons from history. IEEE Annals of the History of Computing*. Vol, 15. No. 1. Issue 1 pp. 44-47, 1993, and Issue 4 7-26. 1993. One of the most complete and accurate reviews of the development of electronic check processing.

8. Green, Edwin. *Banking. An Illustrated History*. New York: Rizzoli International Publishers, 1989.

9. Giuseppi, John. *The Bank of England. A History of its Foundation in 1694*. Chicago: Henry Regnery Company, 1966.

10. Hammond, Bray. *Banks and Politics in America from the Revolution*

to the Civil War. New Jersey: Princeton University Press 1957.

11. Josset, C.R. *Money in Great Britain and Ireland.* Great Britain: David & Charles Newton Abbot, 1971.

12. Kemmerer, Edwin Walter. *Money. The Principles of Money and Their Exemplification in Outstanding Chapters of Monetary History.* New York: The Macmillan Company, 1935.

13. Kuhn, Hermann. *Conservation and Restoration of Works of Art and Antiquities – Volume 1.* London: Butterworths, 1986.

14. Kurtsman, Joel. *The Death of Money.* New York: Simon & Schuster, 1993.

15. Nickell, Joe. *Pen, Ink, & Evidence.* The University Press of Kentucky, 1990. A comprehensive analysis of handwriting and writing materials. Interesting chapters on watermarks, document examination, and forgery.

16. Oldfield, Homer R. *King of the Seven Dwarfs. General Electric's Ambiguous Challenge to the Computer Industry.* Los Alamitos: CA IEEE Computer Society Press, 1996.

17. Hudson, Michael (editor), *Merchants of Misery. How Corporate America Profits From Poverty.* Monroe, Maine: Common Courage Press, 1996

18. Mary L. King. *The Great American Banking Snafu.* Lexington, Massachusetts, Toronto: D.C. Heath and Company, 1985.

19. Morgan, E. Victor. *A History of Money.* Baltimore, Maryland: Penguin Press, 1965.

20. Nitsche, Roland. *Money.* Collins Publishers. McGraw-Hill Book Company, 1970.

21. Reynard, Michael. How the serious collector should care for and display material. *Autograph Collector's Magazine.* Vol. 6. No. 4, pp. 28,28, March 1991.

22. Reynard, Michael. Preservation of Autographs: Plastic, frames and encapsulation. *Autograph Collector's Magazine.* Vol. 6. No. 4, p. 18, April 1991.

23. Reynard, Michael. *Money Secrets of the Rich and Famous.* New York: Allworth Press, 1999. Fascinating stories of fame and fortune of the rich and famous documented with rare images of checks.

24. Samhaber, Ernst. *Merchants Make History: How Trade Has influenced the Course of History Throughout the World.* New York: The John Day Company, 1964.

25. Shaw, David. *A Pictorial Guide to Cheque Collecting.* Scotland: Cheques Unlimited, 1985. A photographic display of an interesting collection of cheques from England and Scotland.

26. Sowards, Neil (editor). *The Handbook of Check Collecting.* Privately printed by Neil P. Sowards, 548 Home Avenue, Fort Wayne, Indiana 46807-1606, 1975. A nice 97-page spiral bound overview of check collecting that includes chapters on check history and varieties of collectible checks.

27. Spahn, Walter Earl. *The Clearing and Collection of Checks.* New York: The Bankers Publishing Co., 1926.

28. Thomson, Garry, *The Museum Environment.* London: Butterworths, 1988.

29. Vartian, Armen R. *Legal Guide to Buying and Selling Art and Collectibles.* Chicago: Bonus Books, 1997. Informative reference to buying and selling collectibles. Sections dealing with auction houses and dealers are especially useful.

Glossary

Archival state of being free of substances that cause deterioration. Archival paper is free of acid and lignan.

Bank a business establishment at which money is kept for saving or commercial purposes or is invested, supplied for loans, and/or exchanged.

Bank draft an order by one bank on another bank directing payment to a third party.

Bill of exchange a document sold at one place and payable at another place. Typically utilized to transfer currency or specie over long distances.

Cashier manager of payments and receipts in a banking or mercantile business.

Cashier's check a check drawn by a bank on its own funds and signed by a cashier or authorized bank representative.

Certified check a check that is confirmed by the bank on which it is drawn.

Check a written order from a bank to pay money as specified. Further defined in Section 3-104 of the Uniform Commercial Code as having three components: 1) The signature of the maker (drawer); 2) a specified sum of money to the order of the payee, and; 3) to be drawn on a bank and payable on demand.

Check truncation conversion of information on a check into a form of electronic recording after it enters the processing system. Truncation refers to an abbreviated physical handling of check processing.

Clearinghouse voluntary association or corporation that serves as an exchange for members banks to exchange items and make settlements for items drawn on each other.

Code Line, MICR the 0.25-inch (6.35-mm) high area located in the clear band that contains MICR characters. Also known as the MICR band.

Convenience amount value of a check expressed in numbers.

Correspondent bank a bank that maintains an account relationship or exchange service with another bank.

Cheque English spelling for check.

Counter check a check obtained at the counter to be cashed only at the bank of the drawer.

Counterfoil a part of a check that is retained as a record of payment. English term equivalent to "check stub."

Debossment sunken impressions of characters on paper.

Draft an order for payment of money drawn by one person, firm, or bank on another person, firm, or bank.

E-13B most common type of font used in magnetic ink printing consisting of ten numeric charters and four symbols.

Embossment raised impressions of printed characters on paper. Invented in England in 1796.

Encoding imprinting of MICR characters on checks, deposit slips, or other bank documents; also may refer to a magnetized recording of data on the magnetic strip of a bank card.

ERMA acronym for Electronic Recording Machine Accounting, a computerized process to automate banking bookkeeping.

Federal Reserve Bank central bank of the United States, consisting of twelve regional banks, established to maintain reserves, bank notes, and lend money to member banks. The Federal Reserve Banks are also responsible for supervising member banks in their areas and are involved in the setting of national monetary policy.

Font collection of typographic characters with a consistent style

Imprinted revenue a revenue stamp pre-printed on stocks, bonds, tickets, and checks. The most common U.S. imprints are found from1867 to 1883, and again from 1898 to 1901. British imprints are also very common. U.S. imprints are usually orange. British imprints are normally red.

Investment bank an individual or institution that serves as an underwriter or agent for corporations or municipalities issuing securities. Unlike traditional banks, investment banks do not accept deposits from or provide loans to individuals. Also referred to as investment banker.

Lamination process of reinforcing fragile paper, usually with thin, translucent or transparent sheets. Some forms of lamination are considered unacceptable as conservation methods because of potential damage from high heat and pressure during application, instability of the lamination material, or difficulty in removing the laminated item, especially long after the treatment was performed.

Legal amount value of a check expressed in text. If this value differs from the convenience amount, the legal amount takes precedence.

Lignan natural component of plants that contributes to deterioration of paper.

Logo an identifying symbol used to identify, advertise, and/or promote an organization, event, product, or service.

Magnetic ink usually consists of printer's ink with the addition of oxide particles.

MICR acronym for Magnetic Ink Character Recognition. Consists of magnetic ink printed characters that can be recognized by high-speed magnetic and/or optical character recognition (OCR) equipment.

Manuscript check a check without printing that is completely hand-written.

MICR line also known as the MICR band.

Money order an order issued by a post office or bank for payment of a specified sum at another office.

OCR acronym for Optical Character Recognition; technnique for reading a font using optical methods.

Payee the recipient of payment, usually from cash, check, money order, or promissory note.

Payor the person, company, or regulatory body responsible for making payment to a recipient.

Promissory note an unconditional promise to pay a specified amount at a certain time.

Recto front

Revenue stamp an adhesive stamp attached to stocks, bonds, and other financial documents signifying a tax paid to either a country or state.

Routing number numbering system that identifies a specific bank.

Safety paper highly calendered bond paper that has a surface design and/or hidden warning to identify an attempt at fraudulent alteration.

Scrip pay currency or promise to pay issued for temporary use in an emergency.

Sight draft draft payable on presentation.

Time draft draft payable a specific number of days after date of the draft or presentation to the drawer.

Transit number the U.S. fractional number located in the upper right corner of a check. The numerator is the identification code of the bank against which the check is drawn and the denominator is the Federal Reserve district routing symbol.

Traveler's check draft issued by a bank or other financial institution payable on presentation by any correspondent of the issuer.

Verso backside.

Warrant form of a draft that may be convertible into a negotiable instrument. A warrant authorizes a bank or person to pay or deliver to a third party. Banks consider warrants to be "cash items."

Watermark a defined image or pattern on paper that appears light when the paper is viewed by transmitted light; a digital watermark is an identification code or bit pattern that is embedded into audio, video, or image data.

Acknowledgements

The author expresses gratitude to:
Robert D. Hohertz
George T. Jacobi
Eric Jackson
Michael Mahler
H. R. Oldfield
Roger Outing
Roger Patterson
Society of Paper Money Collectors
Morris Steinberg

Index